THE PLAYHOUSE ON THE PARK

A History of the Devonshire Park Theatre
Eastbourne

THE PLAYHOUSE ON THE PARK

by

Edward Thomas

THE FRIENDS OF THE DEVONSHIRE PARK THEATRE
Devonshire Park Theatre, Compton Street,
Eastbourne, East Sussex BN21 4JS

By the same author

Slices of a Time	Janus Publishing	1993
No Treat on Offer	New Millennium	1996

First published in Great Britain 1997
by The Friends of the Devonshire Park Theatre

ISBN 0 9531765 0 9

Printed and bound in England by
Manor Park Press, Eastbourne, East Sussex

Acknowledgments

Extract from *Tour de Farce,* Copyright ©1992, by Brian Rix reproduced by permission of Hodder and Stoughton Limited.

Extract from *According to Dora,* ©Dora Bryan 1987, reproduced by permission of the author.

Excerpts from *Eastbourne Gazette* and *Herald* reproduced with kind permission of T R Beckett Limited.

The author further acknowledges information taken from *Wartime Eastbourne* by George Humphrey, published by Beckett Features, 1989, and advice from Richard Crook RIBA, AA Dipl. FRSA on the theatre's architectural history.

He also wishes to recognise invaluable help received from the staff of Eastbourne Central Reference Library.

Front and back cover photographs by Brian Carr.

This book is dedicated to past and present

actresses

research helpers

front-of-house staff

actors

members of the Friends

hoofers

producers

stage crew

writers

directors

programme lenders

audience members

managers

without whose stories there would be no story – only history

Contents

Preface

One Sunday morning in May 1958 we set off from home in Hackney and drove in my father's old 1939 Wolsley to Eastbourne for the day. At the age of fourteen I was to be provided with my earliest memories of the resort.

I recall sitting on the Wish Tower slopes and taking note of the theatre scene. Two months earlier I had worked backstage in a production of *Our Town* at Hackney Downs School, following which, I was hooked. If I went anywhere now, I would pay close attention to what was on at theatres.

Here on the Wish Tower slopes I noted that there was a theatre on the pier. Somebody called Sandy Powell was in it. When I got back to my parents, still at base camp on the beach, I asked them if they had ever heard of Sandy Powell. They laughed and said yes.

On the way back to them I had spotted another theatre poster. It advertised something on at a place called the Devonshire Park Theatre. I did not retain the name of the play but I certainly knew the star of it. Peter Butterworth was often on children's television. He was in a programme called *Peter's Troubles*, whose opening shot was of the man trying to boil a kettle over a candle.

So Peter Butterworth was appearing that coming week at this theatre. His wife whom I had vaguely heard of, Janet Brown, was appearing with him.

Nearly forty years later, after I had been asked to write a history of the Devonshire Park Theatre, I dug around in the archives - the cleaning cupboard at the back of the stalls - hoping to find the programme for the play I had seen advertised. There it was. Week commencing 26 May 1958: *Odd Man Out*. A three-hander only, it featured Peter Butterworth, Janet Brown and David Stoll. The satisfaction was enormous. I had come full circle.

On with the show.

Edward Thomas
Eastbourne
September 1997

I

Overture and Beginnings

1884. It was the birth year of personalities as diverse as writers Ivy Compton Burnett and Damon Runyon, film maker Robert Flaherty, painter Modigliani and politicians Emmanuel Shinwell and Harry S Truman. The Fabian Society came into being. Oscar Wilde reached his thirtieth birthday and married Constance Lloyd. The Olympia exhibition centre opened in London. During the spring a nine year-old lad presented his parents with a scathing report from the headmaster of St George's School, Ascot. Winston Spencer Churchill was described as a boy who 'cannot be trusted to behave anywhere.'

On the south coast a new building was in place on the corner of Compton Street and Hardwick Road, Eastbourne. It had been commissioned by the Devonshire Park and Baths Company and designed by Henry Currey. It had taken two years to build.

In May an application for a theatre license was heard before the County Magistrates. At the hearing Henry Currey made a long speech to assist the application and said: 'I am an architect and surveyor, and have had great experience in the superintendence of theatres under the Metropolitan Board of Works.' Currey went on to emphasise the safety aspects of the building by pointing out that 'beyond the ordinary entrances there are four emergency exits.'

The license was granted and the first performance at the Devonshire Park Theatre took place on Monday 2 June 1884. Two days later the Eastbourne Gazette reported on the event.

'The building was crowded in every part and after the band played the opening overture, the sparkling comedietta *The Day After The Wedding* was enacted. After this Mr G M Wood delivered the opening address during which he introduced the Manager, Mr A Standen Triggs and the architect. After this the play *David Garrick* was then proceeded with, the leading character being taken by Mr G M Wood.'

Henry Currey had become the architect to the 7th Duke of Devonshire, thereby involved in one of his most significant works, that of laying out the building estate at Eastbourne. As with another Currey building, St Thomas' Hospital, London, the theatre was to be Italianate in style. This had become Currey's preference following an extensive tour of Italy where he had been impressed by the overall architectural style.

Currey built the theatre on a sloping site, the stalls below entrance level, the facade flanked by white stuccoed Italianate towers with pyramid roofs. The towers served as incombustible emergency staircases – a new concept following fires at several London theatres. At the top of each tower was set a large water tank attached to a hydrant as an added precaution against fire risk.

The entrance foyer was covered by a richly decorated dome and the intimate auditorium included two balconies adorned with delicate plasterwork and columns. The walls and saucer-domed ceiling over the entire auditorium were covered in decorative plasterwork with scrolls, cherubs and caryatids by Schmidt of Holloway. Seating capacity for 955 people was installed.

There had been rumblings as to the need for the Devonshire Park Theatre at all. Eastbourne had seen the opening a year earlier of the Theatre Royal – eventually to become the Royal Hippodrome – in Seaside Road. But the Devonshire Park and Baths Company, with the Duke of Devonshire as a major shareholder, had been determined. Devonshire Park was being built up as a recreation and cultural centre with the building now known as the Winter Garden already in place. The company envisaged a new theatre in the south-east corner of the park as the completion of its objective. In the preceding years local press commentators had observed that Eastbourne had no attractive venue purely for the presentation of dramatic performance. Now the town had two.

The opening week's entertainment was in the hands of the Garrick Company. It presented a series of different productions following the opening night. Tuesday 3 June saw Goldsmith's *She Stoops To Conquer*. On the following evening *David Garrick*, which appears to have been long enough for a complete entertainment, was repeated. *Heir At Law* was enacted on the Thursday and Saturday evenings and *The Belle's Stratagem* was performed on the Friday.

Touring companies were to provide the fare from the start. The Garrick Company moved out and the Strand Theatre Company moved in for the second week of the Devonshire Park Theatre's operation. Led by Miss Ada Swanborough who was in command of the Strand Theatre in London's Aldwych, she brought two productions for the week's presentation.

The new theatre moved swiftly into its first summer and the Eastbourne Gazette of 9 July 1884 picked up on what it considered to be Standen Triggs' policy.

'The early production of Mr Gilbert's whimsical allegory of the *Princess Ida*, or *Castle Adamant*, at the Devonshire Park Theatre, shows how anxious the manager is to introduce the greatest novelties to Eastbourne.'

The theatre was barely two months old when the problem of box office returns was first noted. Reported the Gazette, 6 August:

'On Thursday, Friday and Saturday evenings, Mr Charles du Val, the celebrated humorist, appeared in the Park Theatre with his amusing entertainment entitled *Odds And Ends*. On each occasion Mr du Val sustained that very wide reputation which he has gained as a humorist and character artiste of the first rank. The audience were not so large as we should liked to have seen there, but we attribute this to the remarkably hot weather, which naturally leads visitors to prefer outdoor attractions.'

Plus ca change...

There were no holds barred if a reviewer thought a production was not up to scratch. On the afternoon of Saturday 11 February 1889, a performance of *Cousin Charlie* was given. The attack was scathing, especially on one actress who 'dried' constantly. The producer, Edmeades Milne was moved to add a footnote to the review.

'Miss Marsden, who took the part of Nora, at the final rehearsal on Saturday morning, appeared to know her lines very well indeed, but at the public performance her memory was entirely at fault. In all my experience I have never known such an extraordinary case of what may be called stage fright.'

Enigmatic titles were the order of the day. Three plays presented in the spring of 1889 were called respectively: *Kleptomania, Tares* and *Fritz*. The Lyceum Theatre Company visited the Park on 1 July 1889. The company was run by Henry Irving and Ellen Terry. Great disappointment was expressed in the local press that the couple were not appearing with them. Perhaps out of pique the critic gave a sniffy notice to one who was: Sir John Martin Harvey.

In the review of *Aesop's Fables* in October, an early example of an interview appears in the press, with its leading actor, Mr W S Penley. He was clearly wanting greater things from his career.

"You mustn't run away with the idea that I want to play Othello or Romeo. I am quite aware of my artistic limitations. I shall always be a comic actor, but I don't see why I need remain a farcical comedian. I shall make no sudden, abrupt change. My aim is to get parts into which I can gradually infuse genuine character, and go on doing so until I can find the measure of mingled comedy and pathos I have power to express. I am sick of this eternal grinning through a horse collar, and am certain that I can do something better. Anyhow, I mean to try. I shall go into management directly *Aesop's Fables* stops running, and am now busy negotiating for a theatre. If I can't find one ready made, I am going to grow one."

If he did not grow a theatre, we shall see how, within five years, he grew money from a sensational comedy hit still popular over one hundred years later.

In December 1889, the Eastbourne Amateur Operatic Society – not the forerunner of that formed twenty years later – presented *The Pirates of Penzance*. Acting the part of the Pirate King was A Standen Triggs. The press review indicated that the theatre manager was himself no mean hoofer: a tradition that would continue with his successors down the ages. The Pirate King's song, declared the Eastbourne Gazette critic:

'...was given by Mr Standen Triggs, our local impressario. His fine baritone voice enabled him to render it well and worthily. It was all the more effective by reason of his excellent stage presence and his becomingly bold and spirited bearing. The applause that followed from all parts of the house was hearty and unstinted.'

Indeed the customers found favour in general with the critic.

'As to the audience last night, it was enthusiastic without being boisterous, and may be said with truth to have included the *elite* of the town.'

Nor were the reviewers slow to point out if script and performance failed to contain the ring of truth. In February 1894 the critic had his doubts about Mr T B Thalberg who played the title role of *Captain Swift*.

'He was perhaps a trifle too refined in manner for the Australian bushranger, though that may be the fault of the author in fitting the part with language more adapted to the drawing room than to the Australian bush.'

It was, however, in the area of audience behaviour that the reviewers were at their most censorious. Reporting on the first nighters of a Pinero play on 6 August 1894, the critic fired off.

THE SEASON.

MR, HENRY IRVING AND MISS ELLEN TERRY AT EASTBOURNE.

THEY ATTEND THE PARK THEATRE

MR. IRVING'S SON ACTING IN "A BUNCH OF VIOLETS."

Last night Mr. Henry Irving and Miss Ellen Terry drove from the Albion Hotel to the Devonshire Park Theatre, arriving at eight o'clock. There they were received by the Managing Director (Mr. A. Standen Triggs), who escorted them to seats in the front row of the orchestra stalls. Recognising the distinguished visitors, the audience gave them a cordial and respectful welcome. Mr. Irving modestly suggested to Mr. Triggs that the applause arose from the people desiring that the performance should begin; but the worthy Managing Director could not assent to this. There was a crowded and fashionable audience. After the performance of "A Bunch of Violets,"—in which Mr. Irving's son took part—Miss Terry remained some time in the vestibule conversing with Mr. Triggs.

Eastbourne Gazette, 29 August 1894

'There is no doubt a certain prejudice in Eastbourne against *The Second Mrs Tanqueray*, but it is almost entirely confined to those who have not seen the play and have imbibed their ideas from weak and foolish people who are ready to accept any idle tale that is told them. For the most part the audience on Monday night was sympathetic. I was perforce obliged to hear a dragon-like female and an equally unpleasing man audibly expressing their disapprobation. When Paula Tanqueray exclaimed: "What a beast I am!", these kindly creatures expressed their concurrence. Even when she spoke of self-destruction, they amiably murmured: "The best thing she could do".'

Filling the part of Aubrey Tanqueray 'with dignity and ability' quoth the reviewer, was the Sussex amateur cricketer, Mr C Aubrey Smith.

Four decades later, Sir C

Aubrey and his wife, Dame May Whitty, would become part of the English cricketing colony of Hollywood's golden era.

Later the same August theatrical royalty came to town to mark the occasion of Lawrence Irving's appearance in *A Bunch of Violets* by Sidney Grundy. The disappointment of five years earlier was assuaged when Lawrence's father, Henry Irving, accompanied by Ellen Terry, arrived to a dignified welcome.

On 24 September 1894 the late century equivalent of the hottest ticket in town came to Eastbourne. Brandon Thomas had written *Charley's Aunt* two years earlier and already one production had been seen at the Devonshire Park Theatre. Mr W S Penley, whom the Gazette had interviewed five years earlier, had achieved his aim of going into management. He had also persuaded Brandon Thomas to sell him the rights, with financial results astounding for the period. The Eastbourne Gazette was effusive in its praise of the production.

'It is very difficult to realise the mental condition of the man who confessed he could see no fun in *Charley's Aunt*. Certainly it has nothing in common with the run of pieces that are in some theatres just now the rage. The word 'society' does not once occur in the dialogue, there is no attempt at smart writing, no Oscar Wilde epigrammatic paradoxes, no satirical reflections of the Sidney Grundy type, no questionable suggestions, no Ibsenite ghoulishness. It is simply a pure little comedy, of a refined type, yet teeming from beginning to end with provocatives to merriment; and, taken altogether, is probably the best modern piece of its class. The fact that Mr Penley, who purchased Mr Brandon Thomas (the author's) rights, has up to the present time netted the prodigious sum of £94,000, is a sufficient proof of its immense popularity – a popularity that even seems still to grow day by day.

"A GAIETY GIRL" AT THE PARK THEATRE.

A COMPANY OF FIFTY TWO.

The *pas seul* in the first act will be given by Miss Topsy Sinden, and the Carnival Dance in the second act by Topsy Sinden and Madge Russell The following card left at this office is doubtless intended for the gilded youth of Eastbourne:

Devonshire Park Theatre, Eastbourne.
"A GAIETY GIRL"
At Home,
Monday, July 23rd, and every Evening during the Week.
Will be pleased to see you.

Eastbourne Gazette, 18 July 1894

It should be realised that by the last years of the nineteenth century the general cultural scene in Eastbourne was flourishing. As with the Devonshire Park Theatre, a different play and company arrived each week at the Theatre Royal, Seaside Road. At the Devonshire Park Pavilion, in the building now known as the Winter Garden, classical performances were regularly given. In the last week of October 1894, while Charles Wyndham's company was appearing at the DPT in *The Bauble Shop*, the Devonshire Park Pavilion was hosting a recital by Sir Charles Halle.

During the same week the Eastbourne Gazette gave a boost to the evangelistic power of the playhouse.

'We really cannot see why a certain class of pessimist should condemn theatre-going when such pieces as *The Bauble Shop*, *The Dancing Girls*, *The Masqueraders*, *Judah*, and similar pieces of equally good moral tone are in evidence. Pieces of this description cannot be calculated to teach other than good, and many a person lacking preaching powers would no doubt give much were he able to impress his congregation of their evil ways as vividly and as powerfully as does Mr Henry Arthur Jones in his plays such as *The Bauble Shop*.'

The same enthusiasm abounded in a preview of a new musical farce which the critic had seen along the coast before its arrival at the Devonshire Park Theatre in April 1897.

'*Skipped By The Light of The Moon* by G R Sims was last week performed at the Theatre Royal, Brighton, and immensely amused a large audience. The house simply roared at the grotesque humour of the scene in which Obadiah Dingle and Augustus Crackle 'skip by the light of the moon' only to find themselves in more serious trouble. The whole performance is an unbroken laugh and therefore it may fairly be regarded as a triumph for author, composer and interpreters.'

Although no immediate threat was imminent, signs of eventual competition for the theatre came in an unexpected form. Earlier in the spring a silent motion picture had been made for the first time of a heavyweight championship fight. It had taken place in Carson City, Nevada, between the Cornishman, Bob Fitzsimmons and 'Gentleman' Jim Corbett.

Meanwhile, the music world was mourning the death of Brahms in Vienna in April.

The first show of 1899 was *The Belle of New York* presented by Williamson and Musgrove's Company direct from the Shaftesbury Theatre, London. Said the Eastbourne Gazette:

'There was a big house, the reception of the piece was enthusiastic, and there is every prospect of the visit of our American cousins being a prosperous one.'

While the touring shows came and went, the political scene in Eastbourne was intense with discussion about the introduction of tramways. The good citizens of The Avenue wanted none of them and references were made in the correspondence columns to the 'snooty Uppertonians'. A group describing itself as 'the inhabitants of Pevensey Road' took a different line. They wanted trams as soon as possible. The Pevensey Road route would be preferable to one through Seaside Road partly because 'by its adoption the dangerous Albion corner will be avoided, and there will be no interference with carriages stopping at the Theatre Royal'.

The occasional production came along to reflect an international angle on the period, especially one involving Britain, still earnestly building its Empire. The press notice of a production in May 1899 included a note of positive alarm for what patrons could expect the following week in their theatre-going.

'*A Life of Pleasure* coming to the Devonshire Park Theatre next week is a military drama written by the late Sir Augustus Harris and Mr Henry Pettitt. Part of the action takes place in Burma, and in the fight with the British soldiers the Maxim gun is introduced, firing from six to seven hundred shots per minute. This scene will be of peculiar interest just now, as it was by the use of guns exactly like those used in *A Life of Pleasure* that the British troops obtained such a decisive victory over their opponents at Omdurman.'

When the play arrived in Eastbourne, the critic was ecstatic. Production and number of players appeared to give young audiences a foretaste of what to expect from Cecil B de Mille in another medium in years to come. But how did it all fit on to the stage of the Devonshire Park Theatre?

'The love story is admirably worked out, the interest culminating in the exceptionally exciting fourth act, the scene of which is laid in Burma. Here we are introduced to the camp of a small band of British soldiers, who are expecting an attack by natives. The arrival of letters is followed by the advent of much-needed reinforcements. The troops commence their march. Before they reach the scene of action, however, they are confronted by a yawning chasm, the bridge which spans it having been dashed to pieces by the natives. The soldiers at once start the work of reconstruction, but are almost simultaneously attacked, and it is not until after a severe fight, during which the Maxim guns brought on to the stage do useful work, that the enemy is repulsed. This representation is admirably managed, and aroused the large audience at the Devonshire Park Theatre on Monday evening to enthusiasm; but it is not the only remarkable feature of the drama. Other set scenes are equally fine, those of the Lawn at Skindles and of the Houseboat on the Thames at night being, in particular, perfect stage pictures. The Irish locale of the first act is very properly suggested, and another scene represents the brilliantly illuminated vestibule of the London Empire Music Hall. In addition to spending money lavishly in the mounting of *A Life of Pleasure*, Mr Henry Dundas has shown great discretion in the selection of his company. In a cast of forty-two characters it is of course difficult to particularise.'

The Maxim gun may have proved too much for the DPT. It closed for a short period. However, before the summer season began in June, it played host to one or two single evenings of entertainment. For example, 14 June 1899:

'The visits of the world-renowned Mr Albert Chevalier are always welcome; and we hope that a very large audience will be assembled at the Devonshire Park Theatre this (Wednesday) evening.'

5 July 1899 saw the renovation of the Floral Hall completed and its

reopening as a Summer and Winter Garden. Later in the month the town welcomed with great pageantry the Prince of Wales, the future King Edward VII, to visit the Sussex Agricultural Show.

Eastbourne braced itself in September for another new play by Arthur Wing Pinero. The stir that had been caused with the arrival of *The Second Mrs Tanqueray* created apprehension by the impending presentation of *The Gay Lord Quex*. The alarm was raised in the Eastbourne Gazette on 13 September 1899 and the reckoning came a week later. The critic's words probably caused a sigh of relief in the town.

'Mr Pinero had the good fortune to have his play denounced by a Bishop (of Wakefield), which of course at once gave it a 'boom', the effect of which was not lessened by his Lordship's admission that he had not even seen the piece. Naturally it was imagined that there was something dreadfully improper in it, and the public rushed in thousands to see it. Shall we say that they were agreeably – or disagreeably – disappointed *(cela depend)* at finding that there is absolutely nothing in it to raise a blush on the cheek of the most modest of maidens.'

The Prince of Wales' visit to Eastbourne in July was followed three months later by an actress not unconnected with the Royal household. The announcement came in the Eastbourne Gazette on 20 September 1899.

'MRS LANGTRY. This celebrated actress will give a special matinee (musical and dramatic) on Tuesday next at the Devonshire Park Theatre. Mrs Langtry will be supported by a number of popular London artists.'

These 'special flying matinees' became a feature adopted by manager Standen Triggs. Artists would come from London for the afternoon and hurry back on the train for their West End performances.

A second innovation instituted by Standen Triggs was the occasional special lecture, also usually delivered at a matinee. One such took place on the afternoon following Lily Langtry's visit. It concerned an issue of the time that would continue to engender debate, including that in the theatre and cinema, in the following century. The Gazette made the announcement.

'Amid all the turmoil caused by the second condemnation of Captain Dreyfuss, it is naturally difficult for those who did not at first take an interest in the case to arrive at the facts. An opportunity of doing so will, however, be afforded at the Devonshire Park Theatre tomorrow (Thursday) afternoon, when Dr Marcel Andre, a Frenchman, will give a full and impartial account of 'L'Affaire', starting from the arrest of the man who has been styled: The Nineteenth Century Martyr.'

A far greater issue was looming on the national horizon and from 4 October 1899 every edition of the Eastbourne Gazette thereafter devoted a special column to the latest update of news of the Boer War.

Meanwhile another matter of conflict still fresh in the public mind was recalled by the announcement on 22 November 1899.

'Mr Charles Neufeld will relate his thrilling adventures in connection with his twelve years' captivity at Khartoum at the Devonshire Park Theatre on Saturday afternoon.'

One wonders if Mr Neufeld looked upon his twelve years' captivity as 'thrilling'.

The troubled year ended at the DPT with a fortnight of plays from Ben Greet's company. They included *Trelawney of the Wells* – another by Pinero, *Money, The Rivals, School For Scandal, Much Ado About Nothing* and *As You Like It.* Residents and visitors alike clearly had a feast of theatre to take them into 1900.

AMUSEMENTS.

DEVONSHIRE PARK THEATRE.

ALBERT CHEVALIER'S RECITAL TO-NIGHT.

HIS NEW "MAFEKING NIGHT" SONG.

Mr. Albert Chevalier is to give another of his inimitable recitals at the Devonshire Park Theatre to-night (Wednesday), which doubtless means, judging by past experience, that the theatre will be filled to repletion with an audience eager to be entertained by the king of coster comedians. This popular comedian is now an established favourite in Eastbourne and his merit is sufficient to secure for him an enthusiastic welcome whenever he comes among us. To-night he will be supported by several artists of recognised ability and will himself appear in several novelties, including his latest hit, the "Mafeking Night" song.

Eastbourne Gazette, 13 June 1900

Carmen came to the DPT a month after news of the relief of Ladysmith. The opera was brought to Eastbourne by the Carl Rosa Company. The Gazette critic was thankful to note that the leading lady's virtue had not been compromised by the character of her title role.

'It is no discredit to Miss Jessie Browning that she fails to give a full realisation of the Carmen the author has painted, for to do so she would have had to lower herself to a depth to which no reputable actress would descend. But she gives full expression to the brilliantly charming music, and as much effect to the acting as is consistent with the preservation of her self-respect.'

During August the Carl Rosa Company made a further visit to the Devonshire Park Theatre. The production was *Faust* and the orchestra baton was held by Eugene Goossens Snr. They were followed a week later by Frank Benson's company. This was a last-minute attraction as the company's projected visit to the Comedie Francaise was cancelled owing to a serious fire at the Paris theatre.

Frank Benson's company had the distinction of being asked each year to celebrate the Shakespeare Anniversary Festival at Stratford-upon-Avon. Expectations ran high of the man. The London *Morning Post* had proclaimed in the debate taking place even then as to the creation of a National Theatre:

'It is to Mr Benson that we must look, for the foundation will be surest when based on a company whose repertoire includes twenty-three of the plays of the greatest genius the world has yet seen.'

The selection Frank Benson brought to Eastbourne for the week of 13 August 1900 were *The Taming of the Shrew, The Merchant of Venice, Twelfth Night, As You Like It* and *She Stoops To Conquer*.

Mrs Benson took the parts of Katharine, Portia and Viola. The cast also included Oscar Ashe, later to create the musical of the East, *Chu Chin Chow.*

The afternoon of Monday 19 November 1900 provided a special occasion which had the theatre so full that Standen Triggs set out rows of chairs in the orchestra pit and even on the stage itself. A lecture was to be given by a correspondent of the *Morning Post* who had not long returned from an assignment to cover the Boer War. The nine year-old boy who had received such a bad school report the year the DPT opened had come a long way.

Winston Churchill was still only twenty-six but had already won national recognition as a soldier in the Sudan. Four weeks before his lecture at the Devonshire Park Theatre he had become a Member of Parliament for the first time, representing Oldham. Now he addressed his Eastbourne audience with an illustrated talk on the theme: 'The War as I Saw it.'

He told of his capture and escape from a prison in Pretoria and his listeners gave him their undivided attention.

In pointing to a map he declared: 'This, ladies and gentlemen, is the map of South Africa. Take a good look at it. It belongs to us.' Applause and laughter followed.

He concluded by noting with pleasure that interest in the Boer War had not waned. It showed the people of this country were 'thoroughly awake to the realisation of the value of our possessions, of our colonies, without which we should only be the overcrowded inhabitants of a small and not very fertile island, but with which we should remain the centre and the capital of the greatest and grandest empire that the world has ever seen.'

Eastbourne's theatre crowds wended their way homeward and with nineteenth century sentiments ringing in their ears, they eased into the twentieth less than six weeks later.

II

Enter the Twentieth

It was scarcely hinted at in the Eastbourne press except in a report of a watch-night service heralding 1901. The vicar at a local church referred to the New Century. The first play of the century at the Devonshire Park Theatre was entitled, prophetically enough, *A Royal Family*. It opened on New Year's Eve and was described as 'one of the prettiest comedies of the day'. It was written by Captain Robert Marshall, who always retained his military title on programmes and playbills.

Within a month the real royal family was on the nation's mind. If there had been any doubt that the nineteenth century had ended on 31 December, none lingered twenty-three days later when the Eastbourne Gazette reported the official message.

'January 22, 6.45. Her Majesty the Queen breathed her last at 6.30pm surrounded by her children and grandchildren.'

Local outfitters Henry Evenden of Terminus Road were swift off the mark, advertising – less than ten hours later – mourning clothes on sale for 'Her Late

Entertainments, &c.

DEVONSHIRE PARK
EASTBOURNE.

THE DEATH OF THE QUEEN.

The various Entertainments announced for to-day, Wednesday, Jan. 23rd, in the Floral Hall and Theatre, are withdrawn, and the Institution closed to the Public throughout the day. The Booking Offices will be open at 10 a.m. to-morrow (Thursday), for the return of money paid for booked Seats in connection with the above.

A. STANDEN TRIGGS,
Managing Director.

DEVONSHIRE PARK THEATRE.

PANTOMIME,
From the Grand Theatre, Croydon,
"PUSS IN BOOTS."

MONDAY, JAN. 28TH, and every evening during the Week. *Matinees*: WEDNESDAY & SATURDAY, JANUARY 30TH & FEBRUARY 2ND, at Two p.m.

At Eight each Evening will be presented
MESSRS. E. & O. WINGFIELD'S
GRAND PANTOMIME, entitled
PUSS IN BOOTS; or, The Miller's Legacy.
By George Fearnley and E. W. Bowles.

ARTISTES:
MISS MAUD OTWAY. MISS GRACIE VICAT.
MISS BELL ROWAN. MISS ALMA BRUNTON.
MISS GERTIE ROWAN. MISS HETTIE LEE.
MISS LILY LASSAH. MISS RENEE RAYNE.
MISS A. HOLLINGSWORTH. MISS E. RIVERS.
MISS LILA STANLEY.
MR. J. R. VAL. MR. TOM MURRAY.
MR. ERNEST FULLER. MR. GEO. DANVERS, Jun
MR. GEORGE FERNLEY. MR. TOM NELSON.
MR. DAN CONWAY. MR. RALPH FORSTER.
Specialities by AL. KOMA.
The FAMOUS CONDOS, Japanese Wonders, etc.

Eastbourne Gazette, 23 January 1900

Imperial Majesty Queen Victoria'. Thick black lines separated the columns of the Eastbourne Gazette.

Surprisingly, business as usual was assumed rapidly at the Devonshire Park Theatre. *Puss in Boots* opened only six days after Victoria's death – and before she was laid to rest. The reviewer of the production was at pains to explain the thinking.

'But for the fact that it would have been the means of depriving a number of deserving people temporarily of their means of livelihood, no doubt the theatres generally would have been closed, until after the Royal funeral at least. Consideration for the living, however, overcame the desire to show respect to the illustrious dead, and therefore the theatres were reopened after a short or a longer period as the case might be. The Devonshire Park Theatre arrangements for the season included the production of Messrs E & O Wingfield's Christmas pantomime *Puss in Boots* in the present week, and the theatre was accordingly opened for that purpose on Monday. As might be expected, there was not a large audience but under other circumstances the piece was well calculated to afford abundant amusement.'

Once the funeral of Queen Victoria had taken place, theatre-going settled back into its routine with further companies bringing their productions to the Devonshire Park Theatre. Several months later two special performances were given by Mrs Patrick Campbell in *Mariana*.

A review of the play *Sweet and Twenty*, presented in the week beginning 23 September, included the following note of praise.

'The author has been fortunate in the representation of the boy Chris, for Master Hugh Wakefield behaves exactly like a youngster in real life.'

Master Wakefield re-enters the Devonshire Park story more than fifty years later.

In October 1901 Lillian Herries brought her own company to Eastbourne to perform Pinero's *The Profligate*. It was presented to an audience which was in the opinion of the Eastbourne Gazette 'fully capable of appreciating powerful drama'. So powerful in fact that the critic went on to deliver a grim analysis.

'Playgoers will not need to be reminded in detail of the plot of one of Mr Pinero's most gripping plays. It is enough to say, however, that it is a "wild oats" story. A pure woman marries a man whom she imagines as impeccant as herself. He, well satisfied with his choice, is willing to settle to a life of happiness with his bride. Then comes the terrible crash in the woman's earthly paradise: the entrance into her life of the woman whom her husband has wronged, her terrible estrangement from him, the discovery that she has a male friend who loves her, and who could and would have saved her, and the pitilessness of the whole thing. The wife has been injured and the wife has to forgive. She makes the sacrifice, and the husband takes the punishment.'

Yet another play by Pinero – clearly the Ayckbourn of the day – played a week in February 1902. *Sweet Lavender* starred Edward Terry. On the

Saturday a special 'flying matinee' was presented of a separate piece, which was also featured in the Eastbourne Gazette. Note the acerbic remark about child actors and also the lack of apparent recognition of a public safety aspect with regard to seating arrangements.

'Mr Standen Triggs' special London Matinees invariably succeed in filling the Devonshire Park Theatre, and Saturday afternoon's performance by the Wyndham's Theatre company of *Little Lord Fauntleroy*, notwithstanding its proximity to Mr Edward Terry's visit, proved no exception to the rule. When the curtain rose, the house presented a crowded appearance, even the additional chairs in the gangways being occupied, while many who had not taken the precaution to book their seats in advance had simply to be refused admittance. Miss Marion Terry and Master Vyvian Thomas presented a delightful picture of motherhood and boyhood in their more beautiful aspects. The playgoer learns from bitter experience to detest the customary stage-child. To the engaging personality and intelligence of Master Vyvian Thomas, no more reliable testimony could have been furnished than the delight and keen interest which his acting aroused in the children, who constituted no inconsiderable portion of the audience. Miss Terry's acting must have reached the hearts of all present.'

The end of February saw two performances of *Shockheaded Peter*, Carr and Playfair's musical play presented by the Garrick Theatre Company. Hard on its heels came a week's performance of *A Cigarette Maker's Romance*, with Sir John Martin Harvey in a performance he had just given at Sandringham before the new King, Edward VII and Queen Alexandra.

Direct from the Gaiety Theatre, London at the end of March came *The Toreador*, presented by the George Edwardes Company. Giving rise to it was perhaps the most redundant notice of all time from the reviewer of the Eastbourne Gazette, 31 March 1902.

'Those who were not fortunate enough to reach the Devonshire Park Theatre on Monday night until some ten minutes before the performance began, were disappointed at not being able to obtain admittance. The gratifying (to the management) announcement "full" was posted at the entrance. We were ourselves amongst those left out in the cold, and herein lies our inability to give any detailed account of the piece, or of the performers.'

Did they not arrange press tickets well in advance in those days?

Several companies were now regularly returning to the Devonshire Park Theatre and one of these was led by Emma Hutchinson. For three nights from Monday 14 April she presented the curiously titled *The Mummy and the Humming Bird*. It must have provided a long evening for it was performed in five acts. The local press described it as 'particularly suitable to playgoers in a fashionable town like Eastbourne'. It was also claimed: 'No expense has been spared in the mounting, scenic effects and dresses.'

Another regular visiting company was that run by Charles Frohman. They presented *The Twin Sister* for three nights in May and were led by H B Irving, a son of Sir Henry.

There was great fanfare in the press heralding the three performances by Mr and Mrs Kendal presenting two plays in September. The following month saw another special matinee of *David Garrick* featuring Sir Charles Wyndham, whose name still identifies the London theatre in Charing Cross Road.

As usual for the times, pantomime enthusiasts had to wait until after Christmas – 5 January 1903 – for *The Sleeping Beauty*, presented by Frederick Mouillot's Company. It ran for one week and was followed by a special matinee from the Garrick Theatre. *The Bishop's Wife* starred Arthur Bourchier and Violet Vanbrugh.

The young Benedick in Haidee Gunn's production of *Much Ado About Nothing* was Harcourt Williams, who would still be acting fifty years later and making a name in television drama. Mr Williams also took the title role in *Parthenia* which played in split-week arrangement.

These productions in the week of 19 April 1903 brought the first part of the Devonshire Park Theatre's life to completion. For nineteen years it had enjoyed the exclusive stamp of Henry Currey marked on it. Now it was to close for three months to receive the benefit of refurbishment from another renowned architect.

The directors of the Devonshire Park and Baths Company had resolved to reconstruct and redecorate the theatre. They had decided the work should be carried out in such a manner as to provide for Eastbourne – in their words – one of the handsomest, best ventilated, and most comfortable bijou playhouses to be found in England.

The Eastbourne Gazette was fulsome in its praise of Frank Matcham, the architect who had displayed 'remarkable ingenuity and ability', and Joseph Martin, the builder. On 29 July 1903 the Gazette described the new scene to its readers.

'On entering the theatre one cannot fail to be agreeably surprised with the delightful transformation which has been effected. The balconies, which formerly extended only across the end of the theatre, have been extended to join the boxes which have been erected – two at each side – close to the stage. If the lower balcony had been allowed to come forward too far, it would have had the effect of dwarfing and cramping the interior. But being comparatively narrow, it has no such effect. The handsome rounded columns in front of the boxes are of rich alabaster, and have the effect of imparting that air of dignity and solidity which is so much to be desired.

'From the boxes, the orchestra stalls and the dress circle, access is easily obtained to the foyer, which forms a pleasant lounge. There will be a buffet at which light refreshments will be obtainable; and there will be upholstered settees, seats and tables, for the accommodation of those who resort to this foyer, which is 13 feet wide and over 30 feet long and has windows opening on to the grounds of the Park. (This area is now the circle bar.)

'In the stalls and dress circle the tip-up chairs are upholstered in red – the favourite Rose du Barri hue, which has been chosen for the draperies and carpets.

'The front of the dress circle and the upper circle and other parts of the interior have been richly decorated in cream and gold. Arranged a little below the centre of the ceiling is a gilded festoon of electric lamps and opulent globes. Radiating panels are most artistically painted on the ceiling in colours of delicately graduating softness or richness. The broadening lower ends are charmingly filled in with cupids and floreated designs, and a small framed space in each panel bears the name of some well-known composer.

'Over the front of the proscenium is a painted bust of Shakespeare, flanked by figures paying allegorical homage to the immortal Bard. Below this, in prominent lettering, is the quotation: 'To hold as 'twere the mirror up to nature', taken from *Hamlet*. The lower panels on either side will bear illustrations of art and literature. The drop act, representing one of the most beautiful lake scenes in Italy, is the work of Mr Richard Douglass, the well-known scenic artist.

'In the pit the accommodation has been increased fifty per cent; and a separate entrance has been provided for the gallery. The building will be heated by steam in the winter. The work has been carried out under Mr Matcham's direction by the following firms: structural work, by Mr Joseph Martin, Eastbourne; decorations, Messrs de Jong and Co, London: draperies, Messrs Cranston and Elliott, London; carpets, Messrs Maple and Co, London; seating, Messrs Lazarus and Co, London; electric lighting and heating, Messrs Pearson and Co, Eastbourne.'

Thus after a gap of three months, the Devonshire Park Theatre celebrated with a gala reopening on Friday 31 July 1903. Sir Charles Wyndham presented a revival of *The Second Mrs Tanqueray* with Mrs Patrick Campbell taking the title role. Returning to the role of Aubrey Tanqueray nine years after first playing the part at Eastbourne was C Aubrey Smith. The Eastbourne Gazette reviewer either made a slip or knew a thing or two about the star. He described Mrs Pat in her playing of the part as 'unapproached and unapproachable'.

The reviewer went on to record that during the high season the price of the stalls would be five shillings, to be reduced for the other portion of the year to the usual figure of four shillings.

Given that Eastbourne retained its own workhouse, it is obvious that the delights of the theatre were closed off to a considerable part of its population. Not for nothing did press reviewers constantly refer to the DPT's clientele as 'a fashionable audience'. Often the term appeared in the headline of a write-up.

Not that support was necessarily automatic among the privileged classes.

Religion provided a barrier every bit as powerful as pecuniary circumstances. In September 1903 an open service took place at the Methodist Central Hall, in which a visiting speaker, Mr B Myers from London, addressed the gathering on the dangers common to young people. The first dangers, declared Mr Myers, were popular amusements and amongst those the most pernicious was theatre-going. He had been truly astonished to find that a large number of Christian people were in the habit of supporting theatres by their presence. The meeting's chairman, Alderman Duke, endorsed Mr Myers' remarks and stated they knew something of 'the curse of theatre in Eastbourne'. He was one of those Christian men who thought it was wrong for him to attend a theatre.

One wonders if Mr Myers and the good alderman were ever informed that theatre began in the church.

Meanwhile, for the rich and the not-too-religious, the touring shows continued. A note in the review for *The Liars*, presented by Emma Hutchinson's company in August stated: 'Lady Rosamund was acted by a clever actress, Italia Conti'. In years to come, Miss Conti would found in her own name a stage school that would achieve world renown. In the same week that *The Liars* was being presented, the Old Toll Gate Fields played host to the Wild West Show. Eastbourne had a chance to see Buffalo Bill himself, Colonel William Cody.

At the end of August Lionel Monckton's musical, *A Country Girl*, was presented at the Devonshire Park Theatre by George Dance's company.

Wednesday 9 August 1903 saw a special benefit performance in the Floral Hall to mark twenty years of management by Standen Triggs. It is not clear whether Mr Triggs received the benefit of the proceeds himself.

In October came 'for the first time in Eastbourne' the latest hit from the Duke of York's Theatre, *The Admirable Chrichton.*

The local press expected Monday 11 January 1904 to be the start of 'a red-letter week at the Devonshire Park Theatre'. The occasion was the premiere of a play entitled *Sunday*, starring the celebrated husband and wife team, Julia Neilson and Fred Terry.

A return visit in March 1904 by the Carl Rosa Opera Company drew the following observation in the Gazette.

'Apart from the association of its lofty traditions, the Carl Rosa Opera Company which is appearing this week at the Devonshire Park Theatre – a bijou playhouse admirably suited for operatic performances, both by reason of its good acoustic properties and the comfortable accommodation it affords – can still base its claims to public recognition upon the consistent and high standard of merit which never fails to mark the advent of this admirable combination as a musical event. (All one sentence!) Tonight Eastbourne operagoers have the rare opportunity of hearing Mozart's delightful *Don Giovanni* which is being performed for the first time in this town'.

Frank Benson's company were again 'received with tremendous enthusiasm' in March when they presented a week of different plays including *The Taming of the Shrew* and *The Merchant of Venice*.

Among the presentations in 1904 were *A Chinese Honeymoon*, a musical comedy that featured one of the great stars of the genre, José Collins. Similarly, *Winnie Brook, Widow* presented Ada Reeve in the title role.

The lecture circuit continued apace and in November Captain Robert Scott gave a talk entitled 'Farthest South'. The Devonshire Park Pavilion was so packed that Scott of the Antarctic made a return visit the following February.

1904 was a year of change in Seaside Road. The Theatre Royal closed its doors and reopened on 6 December as the Eastbourne Hippodrome, the 'Royal' to return several years later.

Certain company names appeared with recurring frequency at the Devonshire Park Theatre as the years progressed. Among the regulars were the teams led by Emma Hutchinson and Ben Greet.

The diversions of 1905 at the DPT included the presentation of a Biograph Picture Show on 23 January. It featured the same Colonel Cody who had been seen live on an Eastbourne recreation field two years earlier. The new medium of the silent picture show was beginning to stir excitement.

A special performance in the theatre on Wednesday 8 February was given by John Philip Sousa and his celebrated band during an exhaustive tour of Britain before returning to the United States.

The presentation of *The New Magdalen*, adapted from Wilkie Collins' novel introduced, exceptionally, a special offer to patrons. The Eastbourne Gazette announced on 15 February 1905:

'Miss Lilian Dundas and her London company will first appear at the Devonshire Park Theatre tomorrow (Thursday) evening, when every lady paying for admission will be presented by Miss Dundas and Mr Standen Triggs with a copy of the novel.'

The return of Lily Langtry in March showed that the local press critic was not intimidated by a great theatrical presence if he thought she was not up to the part. At the same time he could not escape being won over in the end.

'Mrs Langtry as Mrs Dering remains to be mentioned. Unfortunately she has chosen a play and a part to which she is not altogether suited. She is effective and vivacious in the comedy scenes, but her true role is that of the femme fatale, not that of the woman of emotions. In *Mrs Dering's Divorce*, she has a part better suited to the genius of Mrs Patrick Campbell, inasmuch as it is one that requires a display of "emotions". When she can be august and display the "grand manner", Mrs Langtry is supreme, but when it comes to emotional acting, she has no opportunity for a fair exhibition of her endowments. But it is always a pleasure to see Mrs Langtry, for she is always ladylike, graceful and beautiful, and – she dresses well.'

A link with that period's past occurred in a Grand Benefit Concert on Thursday 6 April 1905. The programme included the following announcement.

'Mr W H Pennington, the veteran actor and survivor of the Charge of the Light Brigade will recite Tennyson's immortal poem: "The Hero of Balaclava".'

In the same week as Mr Pennington's appearance, a new star was being heralded at the Hippodrome. The Gazette declared: 'First and foremost we must mention Miss Hetty King who bids fair to become a second Vesta Tilley.'

Hetty King's last appearance at the Royal Hippodrome was as late as 1971 when she played the summer season in *The Golden Days of Music Hall.*

If there were constraints of one sort or another not apparent today, the reverse may well have applied in another particular area. Even the title of the comedy presented on May Day 1905 would no longer be risked. *Are You a Mason?* was described as 'the broadest, brightest and most rollicking thing among latter-day theatrical productions.' Part of the plot might appear positively brazen if thus described today.

'The antics of the two men who mistake each other for Masons when, as a matter of fact, neither is "on the square", must be seen to be enjoyed, and the humour will be appreciated equally by Masons and laymen.'

The Managing Director of the Devonshire Park Theatre then pulled off possibly the most impressive coup of his tenure. The news was announced in the Eastbourne Gazette on 31 May 1905.

'Playgoers – residents and visitors – will jointly rejoice to hear that Mr A Standen Triggs has been able to arrange for a visit from Madame Sarah Bernhardt, the world-famed tragedienne. The great five-act play, *La Dame Aux Camilias*, will be the piece produced and it is to be given by Madame Sarah Bernhardt's company at a matinee performance at the Devonshire Park Theatre on Whit Monday, 12 June. Owing to the exceptional expensiveness of this engagement, special prices will be charged, and we would urge the necessity of early booking as a

DEVONSHIRE PARK THEATRE.

MONDAY, JUNE 12th, 1905.

FLYING MATINEE.

Mr. A. Standen Triggs has the honour to announce a PERFORMANCE by

MADAME

SARAH-BERNHARDT

AND HER COMPANY

FROM

THE THEATRE SARAH-BERNHARDT, PARIS.

General Manager: M. Victor Ullman.

crowded house is practically ensured. Tickets may be secured at the Park booking office and at Clift's Music Salon in Gildredge Road.'

The review in the Eastbourne Gazette on 14 June spread over many column inches. It reported that 'Mme Bernhardt, who filled the title role – that of the pale and fair-haired Marguerite Gautier, a white lily, bruised and broken by the storms of adverse Fortune – was received with much enthusiasm when she made her first appearance.'

It is worth noting how expensive the top stalls price was for Mme Bernhardt's performance. The ticket cost was 10/6d. At approximately the same time, notice was given about Queen Alexandra's Cottage Homes, which were places designed for the not-entirely destitute. It was said that 'inmates' should have a weekly income of not less than 4/- and not more than 7/6d. Little wonder that Mme Bernhardt's audience was described yet again as fashionable'.

Undeterred by the Gazette critic, Lily Langtry returned later the same year to appear in *As You Like It* and *The Degenerates*. 1905 ended with a Boxing Day opening of *Oliver Twist* by J Bannister Howard's company.

The play presented on New Year's Day 1906 drew the Eastbourne Gazette critic's blessing.

'Mr Alfred Sutro's severe diatribe against the evils of smart society, *The Walls of Jericho*, proved so acceptable a play when it visited the Devonshire Park Theatre in September last that Mr Standen Triggs was encouraged to arrange for a return visit of Mr Arthur Bourchier's company.

'Frequent repetition has matured the acting of the company; and on Monday night the comedy was given with hardly a flaw worth noting. It should draw crowded houses, inasmuch as it is wholesome, human and illuminating.'

A few weeks later a play set in Tudor times, *Twixt Axe and Crown* featured as the Earl of Devonshire a young actor who was to become renowned in the theatre, Godfrey Tearle.

The occasional lectures continued and on the afternoon of Saturday 24 February 1906 the speaker was Frederick C Selous. It was his name given to the Selous scouts who had led Cecil Rhodes' expedition into South Africa sixteen years earlier.

The art of local criticism in all its vivid creation and its disdain was exemplified in the review of *The Streets of London* presented in October that year. Notice how much more sophisticated 1906 audiences had become compared with their forebears. The critic presents himself, as so often, in the first person plural: the royal 'we'.

'This production is an example of melodrama run mad; a play in which the low comedy parts are nothing more than musical turns sandwiched between good thick slices of blood and thunder. It is an admirable example of the style of entertainment beloved of our parents and grandparents, and causes no small wonderment in the breasts of their immediate descendants that the dear souls could have been so easily entertained.

'We are informed that under the direction of Mr Eade Montefiore *The Streets of London* is approaching its 2000th performance and that the play is "a classic". If frequent repetition alone is the sole standard by which classics are judged, then *The Streets of London* must stand high in the list of imperishable things, but if on the other hand it is judged by modern standards of dramatic creation, we have no hesitation in saying at once that its proper home is the music hall stage. *The Streets of London* as it is now being performed is as like the streets of London as the resemblance of the kangaroo is to the ichthyosaurus. The play is by the Irish dramatist, Dion Boucicault, and those who cannot appreciate caviare will find it a most excellent Irish stew.'

1906 was to be a year ending in significant change. In the autumn A Standen Triggs decided that after twenty-two years' service, it was time to go. He had presided over the Devonshire Park Theatre's inaugural years and had achieved enormous results. Many stars, some of international stature, had come to appear not only at the theatre but in the Floral Hall and the Devonshire Park Pavilion, all under his auspices.

There appears to be no record of a great farewell but by Christmas A Standen Triggs had left with his wife and family to take up residence at Purley in Surrey.

III

The Pantomine King

The announcement was made officially in the Eastbourne Gazette on 21 November 1906. 'The Devonshire Park Theatre is to be under the direction of Messrs Murray King and Clark, the well-known theatrical entrepreneurs of London, who have in the past sent some of the best companies to this handsome playhouse. The prices are to be reduced; and next year some of the principal London successes will be produced here.'

Murray King's connections with the Devonshire Park Theatre stretched back to 1894. In September of that year notice had been taken in the local press of a young man described, a touch enigmatically, in *The Masqueraders*:

'Mr Murray King is a capital example of the empty-headed swell of the Masher type.'

Over the following years at the Park he appeared variously with Marie Tempest, Edna May, Ellaline Terriss and Seymour Hicks. With the latter he spent much of 1901 at the Vaudeville Theatre, London in *Blue-Bell.* He and Charles Clark, with whom he had teamed up at the turn of the century, brought that play to the Devonshire Park in 1904. They had earlier presented *Sweet And Twenty*, in which Master Hugh Wakefield had found such favour for his schoolboy character.

Charles Clark had spent twenty-four years from 1868 as managing director of the Theatre Royal, Colchester. It was under his management that Mrs Patrick Campbell had made her stage debut. The fact came to light when, coincidentally, her daughter, Stella Patrick Campbell, made her own first appearance in a theatre – the Devonshire Park – in May 1907. The occasion was her mother's starring role in *Magda.*

On Christmas Eve 1906 *The Gay Parisienne* was the first production of the new management of Murray King and Clark, which was to remain at the DPT for many years, although the coming first year was to be a trial run for all concerned. King's name in particular would become synonymous with pantomime at Compton Street even long after his management days had ceased. Although they were late for their inaugural Christmas season, they nonetheless established their mark in the genre in the first weeks of 1907. The Eastbourne Gazette was glad to make the announcement on 23 January.

'It is many years since a pantomime was seen at this playhouse, and Messrs Murray King and Clark, in breaking through an old-established

PROGRAMME.

MONDAY, January 21st, and Two Following Nights. Matinee on Wednesday.

MR. MARTIN HARVEY

Supported by Miss N. de SILVA and his Company.

WEDNESDAY EVENING—

A CIGARETTE MAKER'S ROMANCE

By CHARLES HANMAN.
Adapted from Marion Crawford's Novel.

" There is a greater thing than riches on earth—with it the poor man is wealthy ; without it the rich man is poor ; beggars may possess it ; it is not to be bought by Kings —the greatest thing in all the world —"

Count Skariatine	(his original part)	Mr. MARTIN HARVEY
Anton Skariatine	(his Cousin, passing in Russia as Count Skariatine)	Mr. CHARLES J. CAMERON
Christian		Mr. LEONARD CRASKE
Dumnoff	Workers in the Cigarette Factory	Mr. CHARLES GLENNEY
Schmidt		Mr. PHILIP HEWLAND
Heinz		Mr. DENHOLM MUIR
Ikmenieff	(a Lawyer)	Mr. GEORGE COOK
Nicholas	(a Friend of Count Skariatine)	Mr. W. ABBEY
Akulina	(Mistress of the Cigarette Factory)	Miss MARY RORKE
Augusta	(a Servant)	Miss BESSIE ELDER
Anna	Workers in Cigarette Factory	Miss MAUD RIVERS
Viera (her original part)		Niss N. DE SILVA

SYNOPSIS OF SCENERY. PERIOD 1850.

Act 1 - - - - - THE CIGARETTE SHOP IN MUNICH (*W. Hann*)

INTERVAL (10 minutes).

Act 2 - - - - THE COUNT'S LODGINGS AT SCHMIDT'S (*H. Potts*)

INTERVAL (10 minutes).

Act 3 - - - - THE CIGARETTE SHOP

Business Manager ... Mr. FRANK B. O'NEILL
Stage Manager ... Mr. ALFRED RIVERS
For Mr. MARTIN HARVEY
Asst. Stage Director ... ... Mr. F. J. ARLTON
Musical Director Mr. CLEMENS FRANCKENSTEIN

The Stage under the direction of Mr. H. J. LOVEDAY.

Programme of Music.

OVERTURE	" Romeo and Juliet "	*Gounod*
SELECTION	" A Day in Naples "	*G. Byng*
SELECTION	" Ballet Egyptien "	*Luigini*

Thursday, Jan. 24th, for nine nights. Matinees on 28th and Feb. 2nd, Mr. Constant's Grand Pantomime—
"BLUE BEARD." Miss Isa Bowman, Miss Florence Hersee, & Mr. Gus Danby.

January 1907

convention, have determined that they will be justified in so doing, and to this end they have engaged the best pantomime company of Mr Charles Constant. The cast of *Blue-Beard* includes such well-known artists as Miss Isa Bowman, Miss Florence Hersee, one of the most graceful dancers on the stage, and Mr Gus Darby as principal "funny-man". The pantomime will include several speciality turns, including the dancing of the Arabian Troupe of Lady Dancers.'

Blue-Beard played for a total of nine evenings, the longest run in the

Devonshire Park's history thus far. It was well received by a grateful audience. When it was over, the population came back to earth with a bump. Perhaps it was too much of a contrast to follow *Blue-Beard* with Ibsen's *The Master Builder*. The local press did attempt to cushion the blow in promoting it by saying that 'except for its tragic ending, *The Master Builder* is perhaps the lightest and brightest of this remarkable dramatist's work'.

The theatre-goers would have none of it and incurred yet again the wrath of the Gazette critic.

'We have endeavoured to indicate that *The Master Builder* is a play for persons of certain intellectual culture; for those who have the power to wrestle with thought. That the populace are unable to appreciate Ibsen was abundantly evident on Monday night when some of the most profound parts of the play were received with tittering. If these circumstances are an example of what is to be expected by a company touring Ibsen, one can only admire the courage of Mr Leigh Lovell who dares fortune in adventuring to cast pearls to swine.'

Yet it would seem the Eastbourne audiences could never win. When, the following week, they were gripped emotionally and let it show they received another poor notice.

'We believe that there are persons so curiously constructed that they can find actual enjoyment in weeping like fountains: they have that morbidity of temperament that takes an unhealthy delight in the harrowing of hearts. Examples of these curious creatures were decidedly conspicuous on Monday evening at the Devonshire Park Theatre, and the conclusion of the last act of *Under Two Flags* was played to the accompaniment of audible sobs. Indeed, one emotional young lady was so overcome that she had to be assisted out of the theatre, and we can believe that nothing but honest lachrymose enjoyment prevented other ladies from following her.'

On 18 February 1907 a new Devonshire Park Theatre orchestra under the directorship of one, Herr P Tas, made its debut. It consisted of ten musicians and was reported to have given an excellent performance in its inaugural programme. For once the public behaved themselves by according it 'a hearty and gratifying reception.'

That the problem of a poor take at the box office is nothing new was given emphasis in a report on the first night of *As You Like It* on 18 March 1907. Another swipe was made against the audience, not for their behaviour but for not turning up.

'The Glossop-Harris Shakespeare Company opened their week at the Devonshire Park Theatre on Monday night before a much thinner house than their performance deserved. For some reasons it is not to be regretted that Shakespeare is no longer alive, for had he to depend on certain 20th century provincial audiences for a living, his dwelling place would be the workhouse.'

By contrast a few weeks later, the audience was revered, especially a certain section of it. Notice how the gentler terms such as 'senior citizens' or 'members of the third age' had no place in 1907. And, once again, pity about the production!

'It was really refreshing to see the number of old ladies and old gentlemen that assembled at the Devonshire Park Theatre on Monday evening to welcome a play founded on one of the novels of Charles Dickens. Old ladies who are never seen in a theatre, and old gentlemen who go oftener to church than to a place of amusement or of social edification were at the Devonshire Park Theatre to see the David Copperfield and Dan'l Peggotty, the Micawber and Uriah Heep, the Little Em'ly and Mrs Gummidge that Dickens drew. What they really saw was one of the poorest plays that has ever been written on one of Dickens' novels. There is no more of the real David Copperfield in the play than there is in the "Paradiso".'

Thursday 30 May 1907 saw the premiere production of the Eastbourne Amateur Operatic Society. The selected work for its first run of three nights was *Maritana*, the production under the management of Emeric Beaman. The orchestra was conducted by Cuthbert Hawley and the company included a chorus of fifty voices.

The artistic success of the whole production, declared the Gazette, warranted the establishment of the Eastbourne Amateur Operatic Society as a permanent institution.

So it has become. With the addition of 'and Dramatic' to its title (and the deletion of 'Amateur', in April 1936), the Society has continued to perform at the Devonshire Park Theatre, as well as other venues, ever since.

Monday 3 June saw a hands-across-the-sea weekend conclude with a performance of *Niobe*. The Mayor of Boulogne had been in town and his presence was expected at the Devonshire Park Theatre. The French Prime Minister recalled him suddenly and the Mayor hastily arranged for his son and daughter to come from France to take his place.

The Marseillaise and God Save The King were played before and after the performance. Murray King took the leading part and the other half of the managing team, Charles Clark, designed the drawing room set, apparently to marked effect.

At a reception at the Town Hall two evenings earlier, the Mayor of Eastbourne, Alderman Keay, had declared: 'A century ago the people in this part of the country were preparing to repel a French invasion, whereas now they receive French visitors with open arms.'

Three days after *Niobe* was completed, Seymour Hicks returned with a Triple Bill of one-act pieces to play the second half of the week. His co-star was Zena Dare, whose sister Phyllis had also not long before appeared at the DPT.

The then twenty-year old Zena Dare was to decide in 1958 to retire after one further role. Since the role was that of Mrs Higgins, alongside Rex Harrison as her son, in *My Fair Lady*, the retirement was a long time coming. Following five years at Drury Lane, Miss Dare went on tour and did not finish with Mrs Higgins until 1965, by which time she was 78.

The October 1907 production of *The Knave of Hearts* caused a dyspeptic outburst from the Gazette reviewer.

'The indifferent manners of some of the minor men in the play call for some remark. They are enough to harrow one's artistic soul. Thus the detective always takes his walking stick with him when he enters a drawing room, the butler never looks at the person he is addressing, and – mirabile visu! – we behold the astonishing spectacle of a gentleman invited out to an evening of bridge, wearing a black tail dress coat, a white waistcoat and a black tie! I earnestly beg the gentlemen who undertake these impersonations to buy and study carefully a little shilling book entitled "Manners For Men".'

The following week the same critic was rattled not by stage manners but by local apathy.

'According to the special census taken last week, the population of Eastbourne is 50,692 persons. On Monday night about 92 of these went to the Devonshire Park Theatre to see the fairest performance of *Macbeth* – with William Mollison and Evelyn McNay – that has been given there. The remaining 50,600 probably spent the evening indulging in such weaknesses as big dinners, bridge, the Daily Mail, limericks, love-making and diabolo.'

Later the same month came the curious tale of the production based on a manuscript found at Beachy Head. Murray King claimed he was out for an afternoon walk on Sunday 13 October 1907. On the Downland near Beachy Head he saw a parcel entangled in a bush. Upon opening it, he discovered the script of a play. He advertised the finding but no one came forward to claim it. Murray King decided to produce it himself and it was presented under the title of *Princess Mary Jane,* less than a fortnight after he had found it in the bush. It was described as a 'musical melange' and was received well in the press.

The question remained as to how the manuscript had been entangled in a bush on Beachy Head. Was the Gazette critic's tongue firmly embedded in his cheek when he suggested the progenitor 'was so disgusted with his offspring that he cast it from him to the thorns'? He went on to observe that there was no answer but it could be assumed that if Murray King had been in church that fateful Sunday afternoon instead of 'hunting plays on Beachy Head', *Princess Mary Jane* would not have been responsible for 'many merry moments on Monday night'.

There is no doubt that Murray King was a character. He put his inventiveness to good use building a reputation in his first season at the Devonshire Park Theatre. Confirmation of a long lease would not come until the end of the year and would be dependent on results. The content of *Princess Mary Jane* was said to have smacked of musical comedy, knockabout farce, melodrama, and above all pantomime, the latter category of which Murray King was a master. Yet the entire story of the manuscript's discovery appears to have been delivered and taken seriously with not even one reader's letter suggesting it was a hoax.

Murray King continued to pick up brownie points with the theatre's owners, the Devonshire Park and Baths Company. Their predecessor had brought off a coup two years earlier in booking Sarah Bernhardt, and the new management repeated it. The 'special flying matinee' was booked for Friday 15 November 1907 and the Eastbourne Gazette was there.

'Madame Bernhardt's rendering of Adrienne Lecouvreur was of course a stage masterpiece. In her lighter moments she was always sunshiny, her tragedy was of the pathetic order that brings tears to the eyes. Her piquancy was always irresistible, her petulant moods always convincing.

'The financial success of the educational treat afforded by the enterprise of Messrs Murray King and Clark may be gauged when it is remembered that bookings representing some £200 had to be declined owing to want of accommodation.'

There was, however, another dip in box office fortune when Leigh Lovell attempted a further Ibsen play. He it was who had presented *The Master Builder* earlier in the year, in respect of which the reviewer's opprobrium had been raised over audience reaction. The same occurred with the presentation of *Hedda Gabler* in December 1907. Few people came to see it, and those who did misbehaved.

'What are the reasons that the ordinary patrons of the drama in a town like Eastbourne – whose inhabitants may be presumed to boast of at least an average intelligence – absent themselves from the plays of the acknowledged head of modern European drama? Is it that they cannot understand the divine message of Ibsen? I have no hesitation in saying that on the night on which I was present at the performance of *Hedda Gabler*, the majority of the audience was like a tribe of Partridges in the matter of comprehension; indeed in another respect they were worse, for Fielding does not record that Partridge did other than behave himself on his memorable visit to the play. Such was not the case with certain members of the audience who, seeming to look upon *Hedda Gabler* as a foreign farce, frequently gave themselves up to merriment in some of the most pathetic parts of the play.'

Ibsen and Shakespeare apart, the audiences had grown throughout 1907 and the new managers were home and dry. The 11 December press report spelt it out.

'Messrs Murray King and C Clark have managed the Devonshire Park Theatre so successfully that the receipts for the past year have been double what was expected; and we learn that the firm have secured a 21-year lease of the Theatre which they will take over at Christmas entirely.'

Their long-term leaseship began on Boxing Day with Mr F Mouillot's pantomime, *Mother Goose.* The Yuletide attraction was the more welcome because in former years the visits of companies playing in pantomime had generally taken place after the Christmas period had ended.

The version of *Mother Goose* used was that written by Hickory Wood for Drury Lane a few years earlier and which had featured Dan Leno. The company consisted of no fewer than fifty artists. Minnie Love was principal boy; Edie Coolville, principal girl; Percy Cahill, 'a clever comedian' was Dame. The pantomime ran for nine nights with six matinees.

Murray King and Clark thus set to work on long-term plans, continuing to bring different companies to the Park and being responsible for the annual pantomime. *Dick Whittington* was so successful in 1909/10 that following a short tour, it played a further week at the DPT in February. Murray King was Idle Jack. According to the Gazette of 2 February 1910 it had been up against competition of a type perhaps considered surprising today.

'Since its great success here at Christmas, the whole company has been on tour, and has been received with great enthusiasm at each of the towns visited. Despite the counter attraction of the General Election, it has succeeded in doing record business.'

The General Election brought another State Opening of Parliament, and for the first time Eastbournians could see misty moving pictures of it. New kinemas were sprouting and on 21 February, Mansell's Picture Hall and the New Electric Theatre presented pictures of the ceremony, evoking shouts and cheers from the audiences.

Murray King played several roles during 1910 including the Duke of St Jermyn in *Catch of the Season* at Easter, Nathaniel Glover in *Our Flat* and the Caid of El-Kantara in *A Bedoin Beauty*.

The reputation of Murray King and Clark was gaining ground all the time. Their work was being increasingly revered and the local press reported on the richly deserved support they were receiving. Receipts were considerably more than in any previous year, this despite the downturn in most other theatres, allegedly on account of the General Election and King Edward VII's death. In August the Gazette reported that since the 'High Season' had begun, the playhouse had enjoyed overflowing audiences to the extent that 'over 3000 persons have been turned away during the last few weeks.'

The proprietors also took on the Lyceum, Ipswich on a 21-year lease and even went into the motion picture exhibiting business. By November their Picture Theatre de Luxe – Gallery of Illustration in Terminus Road was being widely advertised.

Alongside such activity, they were preparing for their next pantomime, *Babes in the Wood,* which opened on Christmas Eve 1910 with Murray King as the Nurse.

Two days later, on Boxing Night, the West End celebrated a significant event: the grand opening of the London Palladium. The bill included Sir John Martin Harvey, Nellie Wallace, Ella Shields, Ella Retford and Decima Moore.

Perhaps of particular interest that year at the DPT had been the production in April of *The Still Alarm*, written in 1890. The Eastbourne Gazette conjured up a fascinating picture of it.

'An obviously appreciative audience gave the production a most cordial reception on Monday night, the fire scene in the third act – representing the Central Fire Station in New York – calling forth loud applause the moment the curtain rose. The fire station is complete in every detail, showing the system of receiving fire calls, and containing a real steam fire engine and well-trained horses.

'The custom, existing amongst the firemen of many American cities, of singing on returning from a fire, is taken advantage of in this play to introduce some really good glee singing'.

London's Burning was never like this!

1 July 1912 saw a company run by B Iden Payne present *Man And Superman* at the Devonshire Park Theatre. Bernard Shaw was established as a 'social writer' and his work must clearly have presented a contrast to the usual fare produced at the playhouse. On 3 July the Eastbourne Gazette spoke favourably of its star.

'It is impossible to speak too highly of the brilliant acting of Mr Esme Percy, who gives a very forceful representation of the reformer, Jack Tanner. The part is a most difficult one, but not once was Mr Percy found wanting. His trenchant speeches had all the sting essential to the part.

'A motor car – a 10-12 h.p. Belsize – is used in the second act, and this is lent by Messrs E W Lovely & Co of Cavendish Place.'

Between the opening night and the Gazette's publication, the first Royal Command Performance was staged at the Palace Theatre, London. The object was to give official recognition to the work of the music hall. On that evening King George V and Queen Mary watched Harry Tate, Clarice Mayne, Vesta Tilley, Little Tich, George Robey, Wilkie Bard, Anna Pavlova and Harry Lauder.

In a rare interview with the local press, the lesser-known partner in the DPT team, Charles Clark, spoke in December 1912 of the management philosophy.

'We keep the theatre open all the year round. If we closed the place at certain times we might save money. In some seaside places the theatres are not open during the winter, but we have no intention of departing from the policy we have adopted after the fullest consideration.

'The aim we keep steadily in view is to make the public thoroughly aware of the fact that they can depend on seeing at the Devonshire Park Theatre the very best touring companies. We take the year as a whole in estimating our receipts and expenditure, and we feel that for a town to have a theatre open throughout the winter is a tremendous asset.

'Some of the pieces produced are necessarily expensive. For example the Moody Manners Opera Company has 80 people onstage and 26 in the orchestra.

'There are about 400 performances at the Theatre during the year – the doors being open six nights a week with an average of nearly 100 matinees per annum. Every year we have been here has shown an advance and the present year is a long way ahead of the previous record. This is partly due to the fact that during the summer the weather was more favourable for indoor than outdoor entertainments.

'In August and September we have the most expensive companies. With less expensive bookings we might take as much money, but we have always to consider the prestige of the theatre.

'The public taste is still running strongly in the direction of musical comedies and high-class society dramas. The expense involved in the production of many of these pieces is very great – shocking!'

The end of the year report on the team was summed up by the Gazette.

'Murray King and Charles Clark are two of the most able theatrical entrepreneurs in the kingdom and have made their merit known in London as well as in the provinces.'

Mr Murray King

Mr Charles Clark

The Devonshire Park Theatre closed for nearly a month on 15 June 1914 for what the Eastbourne Gazette described as 'thorough renovation'. The pit was enlarged to accommodate an extra 150 people. The pit refreshment counter that had existed was removed although a bar was reopened to cater for the pit and upper circle. The Gazette concluded:

'The whole theatre now presents a charming appearance, and Messrs Murray King and Clark are to be commended on the superior taste which characterises all the arrangements.'

The theatre reopened on Saturday 11 July with a new play entitled *From 9 to 11* by Walter Hackett. It would transfer a few days later to Wyndham's Theatre, London.

Within a month, the First World War had broken out. The town's population learned soon enough of its effects when the endless photos of the local fallen began to be published weekly.

The First World War provides a link with the Devonshire Park Theatre in its most recent past. In the late 1980s the commissionaire still welcoming customers in and helping them to park their cars was the late Mr Mons Lowen. He explained how he had come by his first name. Mr Lowen was one of several children. His father was at the front on the day he received word of his new son's arrival. On the same day he also heard that his brother had been killed at the battle of Mons. He decided to name his new baby after the battle.

There being no physical impact of the war upon the town, all other life, including that of the theatre, kept going. Many more plays immediately destined for the West End came first to the Park. They included *Peg O' My Heart* on 5 October 1914 prior to its run at the Comedy Theatre. Among the cast was A E Matthews who even then would have been in his early forties.

The recruitment drive aspect of Murray King and Clark's pantomime at Christmas 1914 suggests a production on which Joan Littlewood could have based *Oh, What a Lovely War!* many years later.

Norah Dwyer played Dick Whittington and included the songs 'It's a Long Way to Tipperary' and 'We Don't Want to Lose You'. Murray King as Idle Jack provided sketches relating to billeting and recruitment. Yet surprisingly little was made of 'The Hun'. Said the Gazette critic:

'The evil spirit of partisanship has been largely exorcised. The rascally Germans are not let off Scot free, but references to them are too few and far between to be wearisome.'

Noticeably, the pantomime of a year later, in which Murray King played Widow Twankey, bore no reference whatever to the war effort.

It was inevitable that the Devonshire Park Theatre would gear itself to more light-hearted fare, leaving to one side heavy drama. There was more revue, now presented twice-nightly, one example in 1915 being *A Sister to Assist 'Em*. It announced one of the possibly earliest mentions of the Tiller Girls. There were only eight dancers and their routines, as well as the entire show, were produced by John Tiller. The show's star was Fred Emney Snr, father of the refined and heavyweight comedian of the same name.

Pantomimes abounded during the Christmases of the First World War. Not to be outdone, the Summerdown Military Convalescent Hospital presented their own at the Pier Theatre in January 1916. The billing for *Babes in the Wood* declared soberly:

'Captain E Green Foley as Principal Girl,
Private Hubbard as Principal Boy'.

An interesting evening, no doubt!

The War's atmosphere was everywhere. During the same week as the Pier panto the Devonshire Park Theatre was presenting Harry Grattan's *All Scotch*. It was reported that 'a lady and gentleman are inviting 50 wounded Scotchmen *(sic)* to the matinee on Saturday and afterwards entertaining them to tea in the Winter Garden.

In July a musical play came to the DPT which seemed to have a marked effect on Murray King. The play was called *Romance* and was about an Italian opera singer, La Cavallini. It is possible that the substance was based upon an actual Italian prima donna, Lina Cavalieri, then at the height of her career.

The part was taken by Violet Farebrother, whom the present writer recalls when she appeared over forty years later in the premiere production of *The Unexpected Guest* at the Duchess Theatre.

Also in the 1916 *Romance* was Frank Forbes-Robertson. In the first night audience were Fred Terry and Julia Neilson, for whose company Violet Farebrother had frequently been the leading lady.

Murray King happened to be a keen sailor, as enthusiastic about the sea as the theatre. Much of his spare time was spent off the Eastbourne coast. For many years following the production of *Romance* he had a yacht named 'Cavallini'. The question is whether he was inspired by the name alone or by Miss Farebrother's portrayal of the part!

The first glimmers of resident repertory life at the Devonshire Park Theatre appear to be in evidence in the autumn of 1916. Alfred Wareing arrived with a company to undertake a six-week season of plays that included *The Importance of Being Earnest*, *The Second Mrs Tanqueray* and *The Rivals*. The last named, with its competitive connotations, was appropriate during its week's run beginning 6 November. The Pier Theatre had been converted temporarily into a cinema for twice-daily showings of the greatest motion picture thus far made: D W Griffiths' *The Birth of a Nation*.

One of the great musical comedies of the war years, *The Maid of the Mountains* came to the Park for three nights on 7 January 1918. It was presented by George Edwardes' company. The following week saw *Under Cover* presented by and starring Matheson Lang. Then came a return visit by A E Matthews, increasingly gaining star status with his role in *Nothing But the Truth*.

In February 1918 a play came to the Park, heralded by stark warnings. Unfortunately the previewer never got round to specifying its content, and his criticism the following week is blurred beyond clarity.

'We are to have next week at the Park Theatre a very powerful play translated from the French of M Brieux entitled *Damaged Goods*. This is not a play for the young person fresh from the schoolroom, with little knowledge of life and who will be guarded from the temptations and dangers which assail

NEXT WEEK, JANUARY 28th, and EVERY EVENING at 8. Matinees Wed. & Sat. 2.30.

Devonshire Park Theatre : : : Eastbourne.

First Performance in England prior to [illegible] Tuesday, Feb. 5th, at the Savoy Theatre, London.

Mr. A. E. MATTHEWS.

Every Evening at 8 o'clock.
MATINEES—
WEDNESDAY and SATURDAY, 2.30.

GILBERT MILLER presents

"NOTHING but the TRUTH."

A Farcical Comedy in Three Acts.

By JAMES MONTGOMERY, author of "Ready Money."

All Star Cast

A. E. MATTHEWS.
CHARLES GLENNY.
PAUL ARTHUR.
PERCEVAL CLARK.
O. B. CLARENCE.

RENÉE KELLY.
HENRIETTA WATSON
NORAH FLEMING.
MARIE LEMAN.
ZOE GORDON.
DOROTHY MINTO.

All Star Cast

"For Laughing Purposes Only."

Miss RENÉE KELLY.

Every Evening at 8 o'clock.
MATINEES—
WEDNESDAY and SATURDAY, 2.30.

January 1918

those who, less sheltered, have to face the terrible evils of modern social conditions, and who too often fall by the way.

'In *Damaged Goods* we see the triumph of truth over hypocrisy. Things are shown as they really are, and not as we pretend they are. It is a strong indictment against the social evil, and there is very plain speaking.

'It treats of facts which to many women of the mid-Victorian era are absolutely unknown, thanks to the system of complete silence and putting out of sight of the truth in which they have been brought up. The distinguished Frenchman, when he wrote this play, did it with the object of warning his countrymen of a terrible evil. The warning – so we believe – is just as much needed here and now, and it is the true province of the stage to hold the mirror up to nature and to teach a high morality.

'If we could have a crusade against the suggestive indecencies, and alluring sex attractions of many of the modern light pieces and revues, one could understand such an attitude, but they are passed as harmless, while the serious effort to show the effects of vice is considered unbecoming and improper.'

Yes, but what was the play about?

For three nights from 11 March a play with a war theme, *Billeted*, was presented. It was a light comedy about two officers allotted to accommodation in a big old country house and it developed the relationship between them and the old lady who owned it.

On the Wednesday of the same week the Eastbourne Gazette was published as usual. Its readers were faced squarely with the impact of the First World War.

A Sussex Boy was how Edgar Wilbrey was described. On a hot summer's day in 1916 the eighteen year-old had sailed to France to join the British Expeditionary Force. He did not return. But his diaries did. Eastbournians were able to read on that Wednesday in March 1918 how much his home town had meant to him. He expressed his dreams while on the Hindenburg line after an attack.

'I only live for one thing now: to return to those who are so precious to me. The real value of a person – and anything – is not realised until loss is, shall I say, threatened. May God spare me and grant an early peace to all this suffering. I am oh so weary of war. True, war has made me – but I was not made for war. I shall not be happy till I am back again in that most select town of Eastbourne. Often, even now, I visit the old haunts and become absorbed in the exquisite music to be heard there. I enjoy these mental treats, but they set me more longing for the reunion and recommencement of a happy life. But I miss the peals of laughter, the palms, the lanterns, the rustle of silks and satins, the tinkle of dainty coffee cups. Yes, all this I miss – the stimulating joyous air of warmth and happiness of glorious Devonshire Park.'

Eight months later the Armistice was signed. The other Sussex boys – those who had survived – began their homeward journeys. They, like Edgar, may have longed for the peals of laughter, for the exquisite music, for the warmth and happiness of glorious Devonshire Park.

It was waiting for them.

IV

Flappers and These Foolish Things

The eleventh day of the eleventh month in 1918 happened to be a Monday, which meant the start of a new show at the Devonshire Park Theatre. Two days later the Eastbourne Gazette said it all.

'Peace and *High Jinks*. What a happy combination. Messrs Murray King and Clark could not have made better arrangements for Monday night at the Devonshire Park Theatre. Naturally everybody was in the merriest of moods, and *High Jinks* is a musical comedy of that light character which appeals to people in good humour. Everybody wanted to laugh and to relieve pent-up feelings, and they found the jokes and lively music of *High Jinks* the right sort of thing. Rowland Hill and the other members of the company, including dainty Edith Drayson, entered into the spirit of the evening and, though the motion of the evening was disturbed at times by the hilarity of the audience, there was nothing approaching disorder. Officers in large numbers were present, and they forgot for the time being that there had been a war. The whole atmosphere was delightfully free and easy as befitted the occasion, and the crowded audience will always pleasantly associate *High Jinks* with Armistice Night.'

The reverie continued in the weeks ahead. In the lead-up to Murray King and Clark's 1918 Christmas show, it was described one week as 'the great peace pantomime', and the next as 'the gorgeous peace and plenty pantomime.'

Ali Baba and the Forty Thieves opened on Boxing Day. Murray King played Mrs Ali Baba. As far as the wages bill was concerned, caution was thrown to the wind for there were no fewer than forty-eight thieves in the cast apart from any other members of the company.

Peace reigned and the new year continued with further shows pouring in to the Devonshire Park, often still at the rate of two per week with a change on Thursdays. Within a year, however, a personal blow had struck.

Murray King's professional partner of twenty-five years became ill during 1919, and on 16 September Charles Clark died at the age of 64. Legend has it that scarcely a cross word had passed between them, and together with Clark's niece they had shared a contented household at Edinburgh House, Blackwater Road. Perhaps as a tribute the name 'Murray King and Clark' was to continue as that of the sole lessees. Moreover, any new show produced by

Murray King came under the same banner, as in the case of *Cinderella* which opened on Boxing Day 1919.

Not without a certain irony, one of the period's most lavish shows came to the Park the week after Charles Clark's death. *Chu Chin Chow* had played in London throughout the First World War. Now it had come to Eastbourne and suddenly the stilted writing of the Eastbourne Gazette critic vanished from his pen. He declared simply: '*Chu Chin Chow* is the most gorgeous production ever seen at the Devonshire Park Theatre'. Undoubtedly, Charles Clark would have been delighted to see it too.

September 1920 saw what was to be the first of many appearances at the DPT by Phyllis Neilson-Terry. The daughter of Julia Neilson and Fred Terry, she came to the Park with one of her richest successes. She had played Trilby for several years at His Majesty's Theatre, London. Her performance caused the Gazette reviewer to wax lyrical.

'Wonderful! There is no other word sufficiently expressive to describe Miss Neilson-Terry in *Trilby*. Here is a combination of dramatic and musical art which perhaps is unrivalled on the stage today. A charming personality, an artist to her finger tips, a vocalist of remarkable quality and compass.'

The reviewer was also taken with her curtain speech.

'This is my first appearance in Eastbourne, and I only hope you will reserve as warm a place in your hearts for me as I know you have for my dear mummy and daddy.'

Miss Neilson-Terry would return in various roles over the following twenty years. Her long career would include, towards its end, an unlikely vehicle: Richard Burton's mother-in-law in the 1958 film version of *Look Back in Anger*.

Dick Whittington was presented on Boxing Day, the theatre opening after yet another overhaul. It had been closed for only a week in December 1920, during which time work must have been carried out at a furious pace. Redecoration was undertaken in the vestibule, lounges, corridors and much of the auditorium. All the bench seating in the gallery was replaced with cushioned tip-up seats equal to those in the stalls.

The Gazette hoped that the enterprise of the management would meet with due reward. Seat prices would remain the same as before. The paper concluded: 'The interior of the building is diamond-like in its brilliancy, and everyone will appreciate its beauty and comfort.'

Places of entertainment were having to look to their laurels in general. 21 December 1920 saw the grand opening of another plush auditorium: the Picturedrome in Langney Road, now the Curzon. It was described in the press as 'the largest. most luxurious and perfectly equipped picture house on the south coast.' Competition was on.

Meanwhile an issue that had blown up in the press was the debate about bathing and bands being permitted on Sundays. 'Vote for rational Sundays!'

pleaded the Gazette. Those wanting the ban to continue felt they were being ridiculed. 'We're being satirized for our respectability,' they proclaimed. When the final decision was made, the Gazette delivered the resigned note of defeat: 'Sad Sundays to remain.'

A further distinct sign of the times came with the December 1922 production, *Welcome, Stranger*. It had arrived direct from the Lyric, Shaftesbury Avenue following a long run. As though not quite able to believe it, the Gazette announced the star as 'Harry Green (himself)'.

The present writer can recall Mr Green in a revival of the same play in a television production before a live audience in the mid-Fifties. Harry Green was a very funny man who sometimes appeared in the role of the downtrodden Jew. *Welcome, Stranger* was in that vein and it is difficult now to imagine it as acceptable in the Twenties, let alone the Fifties.

What the Devonshire Park Theatre audience saw in December 1922 was a rip-roaring comedy about Isadore Solomon arriving in a small town in New England. One of its residents is an inventor who wants to provide electricity for the town. He does not have the money to do it but Isadore does. The townsfolk will have none of it as it would mean a Jew getting a foothold in the community. Isadore nevertheless battles on to provide the money, the inventor provides the electricity and because of its advantages, the townspeople finally hail Isadore as a hero. Said the Gazette: 'The curtain goes down on a positive glow of gratitude.'

The object of the piece may well have been to draw out anti-semitic prejudice and lay it bare through broad comedy. The writer recalls vividly a particular line. Confronted by one of the town's citizens, Harry Green declared in thick Brooklynese: 'I don't geddit. You don't want an electric light 'cause I'm an Israelite?'

What was not made clear was the townspeople's likely reaction if the scheme for which Isadore put up the money had <u>not</u> been a success.

A significant production of Shaw's *St Joan* was staged in 1925 with Dorothy Holmes-Gore in the title role. Miss Holmes-Gore would become a popular radio actress for many years. Playing Beauchamp, Earl of Warwick, was Francis L Sullivan.

In July of the same year a new play by Frederick Lonsdale arrived at the Park. The local reviewer took a distant view of it.

'*Spring Cleaning*, Lonsdale's satirical play, will appeal to the modern mind. This was evidenced on Monday evening at the Devonshire Park Theatre when the majority of the large audience found the keenest enjoyment in watching modern girls drink many cocktails and smoke many cigarettes and use language which would shock the old-fashioned – or, as we would put it – the respectable mind. We were particularly struck by the fact that when a girl said or did something unconventional – what a mild term! – the feminine members of the audience clapped and shrieked with laughter. They thoroughly enjoyed themselves, for *Spring Cleaning* is crammed full of "unconventional" sayings and actions which the modern mind revels in.'

The paper went on to advise readers that Lilian Christine played the wife, Paul Cavanagh was the husband and Mary Anthony portrayed the Girl of the Streets.

Firmer ground was reached again by Boxing Day when *Goody Two Shoes* opened. Such was Murray King's reputation by now that the review of the pantomime was placed as the lead story in the Eastbourne Gazette and two long columns were devoted to it.

If silent films were beginning to cause moderate worry as far as competition was concerned, an event along the coast in 1926 probably did little to stir hearts. It was in that year in an attic above a flower shop in Hastings that John Logie Baird succeeded in transmitting the world's first television moving pictures. The impact would be a long time coming.

Meanwhile the live shows went on. On 16 May 1927, less than a month after *The Desert Song* first opened at Drury Lane with Harry Welchman and Edith Day, a production of Eden Philpotts' *The Farmer's Wife* came to the Park. After mentioning a host of people in the cast, the critic went on:

'Messrs Robert Coote and Edward Wheatleigh present clever studies of the young men who are in love.'

While the latter name perhaps conveys little, Mr Coote grew to star status. Thirty years later he would create the role of Colonel Pickering in the original Broadway production of *My Fair Lady*.

As the week's run of *The Farmer's Wife* ended, an achievement of world significance was taking place across the Channel. The DPT curtain fell on the Saturday night at approximately the same time as Charles Lindbergh was landing his small aircraft, the Spirit of St Louis, at Le Bourget, becoming the first lone flyer across the Atlantic.

Unlike in the venue's early days, the presentation of a lecture had become a rare event at the Park, but one was given on Friday 4 November 1927. An elegantly gowned Mrs Patrick Campbell addressed the audience on her profession. Much of it was spent in regretting what was gone. The art of the pre-war theatre was passing and the art of acting was diminishing.

'Today there is a great carelessness in speech, and the time devoted to the teaching of correct speaking is very small compared with the time devoted to other subjects.'

Sobering to reflect that such sentiments were being expressed in 1927! Could it be there is nothing new in the belief that standards of the present age are worse than in the previous one?

Christmas 1927 saw *Robinson Crusoe* billed as Murray King's coming-of-age pantomime. For the second consecutive year the review of the production was placed as the lead story in the following week's Gazette.

The management had been at the Devonshire Park Theatre for twenty-one years. It went forward into 1928 with a renewed and extended lease. Although his partner had been dead for eight years, the sole lessee was still to be recognised as Murray King and Clark.

The pantomime was followed by a John Galsworthy play, which gave the Gazette critic an opportunity to express his restlessness.

'The production of *Escape* at the Devonshire Park Theatre provides a welcome change from comedy and farce, of which for some time we have had good measure.'

A procedure had long been adopted of presenting plays for half-weeks only. As a result the eagerly awaited *The Scarlet Pimpernel* played only three nights from Monday 16 April. Fred Terry and Julia Neilson presented the play but disappointment came in the form of Mr Terry's 'sudden indisposition'.

The following week a stir was caused by the lack of publicity given to a visit to the town by a noted silent screen star who had come to see his mother in an Eastbourne hotel. The hotelier declared: 'If we had given it out that Ronald Colman was here, there would have been hundreds of flappers outside the hotel.'

Language is often a matter of the time in which it is used. The word 'flapper' has been out of use for many decades. A further example of what was commonplace at the time emerged in the publicity for *Whispering Gallery*, presented by Premier Plays for three nights from Thursday 3 May. It starred Mary Clare and featured Donald Walcott, described as 'a really clever negro actor.'

Ben Travers' newest farce of the time, *Thark*, came to the DPT in July, followed a week later by one of the many thrillers from the pen of Edgar Wallace, *The Terror*, starring Mary Glynne and Dennis Neilson-Terry (yet another of that family). The Twenties were a time when thrillers came into their own and at one stage Mr Wallace was churning them out at a rate of one per fortnight. In a later age he would have given Barbara Cartland a run for her money.

Before arriving in Eastbourne, *The Terror* had played to more than one million people at London's Lyceum Theatre and the Eastbourne Gazette described its style to perfection. (The present writer can vouch for its authenticity. Four decades later, he played Det Sgt Dobey in a Comedy Club production at the Cripplegate Theatre.)

'The background is an ancient priory with all the effects which inspire bad dreams, and where hysterical women with breathless interest in famous crimes figure in this sort of country hotel. Hooded monks perambulate at night to the accompaniment of uncanny peals of laughter, shots, and criminals in death grips'.

In other words, camp as high as a totem pole.

It was a different scene down the road at the Royal Hippodrome. Playing the same week was a revue entitled *Here's To You* starring Bud Flanagan and Chesney Allen.

Another great comedian came to the Devonshire Park Theatre itself the week following *The Terror*. *Bits and Pieces* starred the so-named prime minister of mirth, Sir George Robey. Indeed the summer of 1928 appears to have been a season of greats. While Barry O'Brien was presenting the play *Lady Luck* at the Park on Monday 20 August, the Winter Garden was playing host to Sir Harry Lauder.

The press reviews of the time would frequently omit essential credits. In the write-up of *Oh Kay!* in September, mention was made of the writers of the book, Guy Bolton and P G Wodehouse, but none of the composer, George Gershwin. In the following week, *Alibi* was presented for the first time but Mrs Christie was not deemed important enough to be recognised as its author. And it would clearly take more than this production for the name of the short, moustachioed Belgian detective to become household, although Francis L Sullivan was credited with having portrayed him.

One incident the Gazette critic did not fail to report took place on the opening night of *Oh Kay!*

'An unrehearsed thrill occurred at the Devonshire Park Theatre on Monday evening. Mr Dennis Rivers, who takes the part of Larry Potter, was doing an acrobatic dance which involved some rapid circular movements. He either misjudged his position or became giddy, for he fell over the edge of the stage into the orchestra, where his fall was broken by one of the musicians. He made a great effort to hoist himself on to the stage again but without success. When he appeared a few minutes afterwards on the stage, he was received with very loud applause.'

Eden and Adelaide Philpotts were known for writing plays with a Cornish setting. The wages bill for managements presenting any of their work was enormous, such was the number of characters with which they fuelled their plots. *Yellow Sands* arrived at the Park on 17 September 1928 and the press reviewer waded through the cast list. Towards the end he noted: 'Miss Jessica Tandy was a pretty Devonshire lass.'

In November *The Night Hawk* starred Olga Lindo. Miss Lindo was an actress who also had her own production company which at one stage had played at the Pier Theatre. In *The Night Hawk*, the part of her young brother was played by Robert Mawdesley. More than twenty years later Mr Mawdesley would create the crusty Walter Gabriel in the first years of *The Archers*. The part would become his swan song, to be taken over on his death in the late Fifties by Chris Gittins.

The Eastbourne Music Festival took place in November. Making personal appearances at the Winter Garden were, on Friday 9, Henry Wood, and, two nights later, Edward Elgar conducting his own *The Dream of Gerontius*.

On Christmas Eve, Murray King presented his twenty-second pantomime, *Aladdin*. As earlier mentioned, Murray King had established another reputation, that of a keen yachtsman. He sailed the 'Cavallini' at every opportunity, often into intrepid waters. On one occasion that year, he sailed from

Newhaven to Rye. As the yacht entered the harbour, a fire broke out on board. Neither he nor his crewman knew how to operate the fire extinguisher. As they both struggled with it, the crewman received the first blast of foam in the face, and promptly fainted. Murray King was left to steer the 'Cavallini', successfully, into port.

Unfortunately 1928 saw the other side of the coin and was a year of tragedy in the area. The Rye lifeboat went down in mountainous seas with the loss of seventeen crew.

1929 gave vent to entertainment in many aspects, nationally and internationally. One of the first projects at the Devonshire Park Theatre was the arrival of Leon M Lion's Galsworthy Repertory Company which played in split week both *Loyalties* and *Justice*. Leon M Lion would figure again in the theatre's history.

A local embarrassment occurred when a February concert at the Winter Garden by Elisabeth Schumann had to be cancelled owing to poor advance take at the box office.

'A.E.B.' in the Eastbourne Gazette was moved by a star of the period who appeared at the DPT in April.

'I was charmed with Miss Clarice Mayne on Monday evening. So were the audience to a man – and a woman. She is a brilliant comedienne and she captivated the Easter holiday audience when she appeared in the Vaudeville Theatre play, *Clara Gibbings*.'

Still in April the Frank Benson farewell tour came to the Park with presentations of *The School For Scandal* and *The Rivals*. Sir Frank and his wife played the Teazles.

The week beginning 13 May 1929 was not without significance. The Eastbourne Amateur Operatic and Dramatic Society had clearly adopted the split week tradition by presenting in the first three days *The Last of Mrs Cheney*, and in the second, *Miss Hook of Holland*. They were up against stiff competition on the Saturday night when Paul Robeson sang to a packed Floral Hall audience.

Mr Robeson received a distinctly grudging review from the local critic who made it clear that he had 'had enough of negro spirituals'. He did have the grace to admit that the audience had 'clamoured for more'. He further reported that the people were not satisfied until he had sung 'Ol' Man River'. It was the song he had delivered every night in *Show Boat*, which had just ended its run at Drury Lane.

From EAODS' point of view, less competition would have arisen two nights earlier. The inaugural dinner of the Motion Picture Academy of Arts and Sciences took place that evening in Los Angeles and the first ever Oscars were presented to Emil Jannings and Janet Gaynor.

Later the same month, Muriel Martin Harvey, daughter of Sir John, starred in Blackmail at the DPT during the week that Ramsay Macdonald became Prime Minister. In Eastbourne the General Election returned Edward Marjoribanks, the present Lord Hailsham's step-brother, as its Member of Parliament.

A storm blew up in the local press during the summer over a proposed aerodrome on the Downs near Friston Church. Also in August, the Royal Hippodrome featured a revue entitled *Hot Ice*. Way down the cast list was a young comedian, Sid Field. Mr Field's son, Nicholas, would appear many years later at the Devonshire Park Theatre during a Newpalm summer season together with his wife, Deborah Watling.

In September Randolph Richards, manager of the Picturedrome declared:

MONDAY, MARCH 31st, 1930, for SIX Nights at 8. Matinees, Wednesday & Saturday at 2.30

Prior to Immediate London Production. **MARTIN HENRY** *presents*

PHYLLIS NEILSON-TERRY

CECIL PARKER, MARGARET YARDE, GEORGE ELTON

and Actual West-End Company in

"THE CRIME AT BLOSSOMS"

A Play in Three Acts by MORDAUNT SHAIRP

Characters in order in which they appear—

Mrs. Woodman	**MISS MARGARET YARDE**
A Laundry Girl	**MISS LUMINA EDWARDS**
Valerie Merryman	**MISS PHYLLIS NEILSON-TERRY**
Christopher Merryman	**MR. CECIL PARKER**
Mrs. Carrington	**MISS MARY HINTON**
Mr. Carrington	**MR. GERALD CLIFTON**
A Young Man	**MR. HENRY MOSS**
Mr. Palmer	**MR. STRINGER DAVIS**
The Rev. Charles Stern	**MR. CLIFFORD PEMBROKE**
Driver of a Char-a-banc	**MR. STRINGER DAVIS**
Young Lady's Mother	**MISS LILA MASON**
A Young Lady	**MISS JOAN BRIERLY**
The Superior Husband	**MR. GERALD CLIFTON**
The Superior Wife	**MISS ELIZABETH VAUGHAN**
The Flapper	**MISS MARY MARTIN HENRY**
The Man with a Concertina	**MR. ROLAND RITCHIE**
A Dear Old Lady	**MISS KATIE JOHNSON**
Her Son	**MR. BASIL SIMPSON**
A Governess	**MISS MONA HOFFE**
" "	**MISS ELSA PALMER**
A Very Late Visitor	**MR. GEORGE ELTON**

THE ACTION OF THE PLAY PASSES IN THE LIVING ROOM OF "BLOSSOMS," AN ELIZABETHAN COTTAGE IN THE VILLAGE OF WHEATFIELDS. About a month elapses between Act 1 and Acts 2 and 3.

The Play Produced by NORMAN MACDERMOTT

Miss Phyllis Neilson-Terry's Dresses by IRA, 79b Wigmore Street, W. Scenery by FRANCIS BULL. Cigarettes by ABDULLA.

PROGRAMME OF MUSIC.

1. Overture ... "ZAMPA" ... *Herold*
2. Selection ... "LA TOSCA" ... *Puccini*
3. Barcarolle ... ... *Offenbach*
4. "Stories of the Vienna Forest" ... *Strauss*

MUSICAL DIRECTOR - - FREDERICK SEYMOUR, L.R.A.M.

Business Manager	CHARLES CLIFFORD
Stage Manager	GERALD CLIFTON
Assistant Stage Manager	HOWELL DAVIES

March 1930

'They will not come to Eastbourne for the time being at any rate, owing to numerous difficulties and considerations'. He was talking about the Talkies. Curiously enough, sound motion pictures had already arrived at a Bexhill cinema.

In the same month Barry O'Brien presented *The Vagabond King* at the DPT starring Eric Woodburn. Many decades later Mr Woodburn would appear as the eccentric Dr Snoddie in the original BBC version of *Dr Finlay's Casebook*. The reviewer liked his performance but was less impressed with his co-star.

'As the lovely Katherine of Vancelles, Cecile Forbes was requisitely charming, but often was unable to restrain a pronounced tendency to overact, a fault which was responsible for the production of some vowels which undoubtedly would have been banned by the BBC Pronunciation Board or the Society of Pure English. If this fault is once conquered, Miss Forbes should be ideal in the part.'

Following one of the earliest productions of Arnold Ridley's *The Ghost Train* in December, Murray King mounted his twenty-third pantomime. Playing Cinderella was Mona Washbourne. In an earlier Fols de Rols season at Hastings, the juvenile lead at the time was Harry Hanson, and Miss Washbourne was the pianist. By the end of the summer the couple were married. Harry Hanson would later form the Court Players, the company resident on Hastings Pier for many years.

Mona Washbourne would go on to an illustrious career. Those privileged to have seen the performance will not forget her as Glenda Jackson's 'lion aunt' in Hugh Whitemore's *Stevie*, about the poet, Stevie Smith. Miss Washbourne would also achieve international fame as Mrs Pearce in Jack L Warner's film version of *My Fair Lady*.

March 1930 saw a visit by the Original Irish Players who performed both *Juno and the Paycock* and *The Plough and the Stars*. Of the former the programme announced: 'Period of the Play, 1922 – during Hostilities between the Free State Government and the Republican Die-Hards'.

Other offerings in 1930 included *The Constant Nymph* and Shaw's *The Apple Cart*. The curiously titled *Scrambled Wives* starred Iris Hoey, and *The Limping Man* featured Franklin Dyall, Mary Merrall and Ronald Simpson – for many years the voice of Soames in the radio versions of *The Forsyte Saga*. In July Tom Arnold and C B Cochrane presented the revue *One Dam Thing After Another.* Not content with a title risqué for the period, each item in the programme was itemised consecutively: First Dam Thing, Second Dam Thing, and so on.

10 November 1931 saw another innovation from Murray King: the start of a six-week season under the title of his own M K C Repertory Company. He decided to try the repertory idea for himself to get away for a while from the endless touring companies. So he brought together a group of actors who would perform a programme including *Ambrose Applejohn's Adventure*, *The Edge O' Beyond, Mary Rose* and *Lavender Ladies*. The last named completed the season on Saturday 14 December, coinciding with the day the former

Temple Grove schoolboy, Group Captain Douglas Bader crashed his fighter plane and lost both legs.

The company Murray King gathered around him included Wilson Barrett who provided the star content. Among the youngsters were Patricia Hayes and Raymond Francis. Bexhill-born Mr Francis was making the first of many appearances at the Devonshire Park Theatre. He was to come to live in Eastbourne and two generations of the famous family would strut the Park boards throughout the years.

The opening night of Murray King's repertory season was a gala event and telegrams were read out from past performers at the theatre including Sybil Thorndike and Cedric Hardwicke. This winter rep season appears not to have been repeated by Murray King himself, although the following summer saw a shorter season by the Jevan Brandon-Thomas Company.

Before their arrival, however, the tours continued apace. One of the first of 1932 was *The Crimes of Burke and Hare* starring Britain's own horror man with a name that could not have been more appropriate, Tod Slaughter. Along with much of the western world, the country was suffering from the Depression, and in February Murray King announced a significant decrease in seat prices.

February 1932

Depression took a different turn at the beginning of April with the shock suicide of Eastbourne's Member of Parliament, Edward Marjoribanks. His step-father found him beside a shotgun at the family estate, Carter Corner's Place, Hailsham.

The following month a familiar name from the previous century arrived at the Park with a Shakespeare Festival. Ben Greet now had 'Sir Philip' attached to the front of his name. Among the week's roles he played Shylock. The Eastbourne Chronicle was not pleased with local response, although the harsh tellings-off from earlier times had subsided into mild admonishment.

'There have been too many spare seats to speak really well for Eastbourne's reputation. There are towns much poorer than Eastbourne which are keen enough to make packed houses the rule. Empty seats reflect on the town, not on the players.'

Then came the Jevan Brandon-Thomas season. Wilson Barrett was in demand again as the star of all the plays, beginning with *John Ferguson* by St John Irvine. The reviewer told readers: 'Among the company who were all excellent and made the most of a gloomy and wordy play were Miss Patricia Hayes and Mr Leonard Sachs.'

The write-up for the following play unwittingly pointed focus to a star not only of the past but one of the future.

'During the first half of their second week at the Devonshire Park Theatre, the Brandon-Thomas season gave clever performances of Miles Malleson's somewhat daring play, *The Fanatics*. This play was not of course written for children, and many adults even found the talk just a little too straight. It will be remembered that *The Fanatics* is a sort of treatise on free love advanced by the modern generation who believe in trial marriages etc. Mr Wilson Barrett gave a convincing picture of the principal exponent, John, and was splendidly supported by his colleagues, particularly by Mr James Mason as Colin.'

If one potential Hollywood Great received cursory mention in 1932, another went almost unremarked. He was not in the billing for Ivor Novello's play *Party* in August, the focus placed justly on its star, Olga Lindo. He was not even referred to in the review. Only one sentence in the advance notice the week before gave evidence of his presence. 'There is a long and distinguished cast including Rex Harrison.'

For four nights in July the theatre was packed for an artist who Joyce Grenfell was to maintain always influenced her own work. Ruth Draper was possibly unique in presenting a one-woman show in the early Thirties. The reviewer considered her performance masterly.

A play about a newspaper office, *Late Night Final*, presented in September provided the first occasion on which a revolving stage had been used in any Eastbourne theatre.

Murray King and Clark's twenty-sixth pantomime, *Mother Goose*, included 'those famous wireless entertainers', Murray Ashford and Edgar Sawyer.

The programme for the February 1933 visit of the Wembley Empire Circus leaves one aghast as to how the participants were all fitted into the theatre building. In addition to the humour arising from the listings, the programme now reads like an animal rights nightmare.

Ben Hur & Partner, Double Riding Act
Tommy the Horse with the Human Brain
Allan Troupe of Maltese and Fox Terriers
Capt John Forest and his Performing Burmese Elephant
Jeff the Boxing Pony
Capt Arthur Overland's Performing Monkeys and Baboons
'Old Bill' the Performing Sea Lion

An intriguing aspect of the programme for Murray King's 1933 pantomime is that it was accompanied by cardboard tinted spectacles, after the style of glasses presented to cinema patrons in the Fifties when attending a film that was in 3-D. The purpose of the glasses is undiscovered.

A week of Variety began on 14 May 1934 starring Harry Tate. The programme included the item: 'First variety appearance by Hughie Green – in clever impersonations'.

The same year saw a production of *Clive of India* featuring Wilfred Babbage and Leslie Dwyer. It was presented by Ena G Lovell, whose name would figure in the DPT's history within a short time. *Clive of India* was on tour and Miss Lovell wondered how to formulate publicity for it when it reached Eastbourne. Her husband, Maurice Jackson, found the answer.

Jackson was a lifetime business associate of the Fols de Rols man, Greatrex Newman. He obtained a John Flag, the banner of the East India Company in Clive's time. He ran it up the flagpole outside the Devonshire Park Theatre but deliberately hoisted it upside down. An irate colonel of the Indian Army spotted it and wrote a furious letter to the local press, thereby highlighting the production. As a result business was boosted substantially.

Murray King's pantomime star continued to shine and his twenty-eighth production, *Jack and the Beanstalk*, at Christmas 1934 was described as 'the best effort he has ever made.'

Plenty was happening in 1935 but for once little of it was going on at the DPT. Following the pantomime, Barry O'Brien presented a London hit, *The Wind and The Rain*. Then the Park theatre shut down without explanation. The field was left to the Royal Hippodrome Theatre, whose own repertory company had been established. It included Miss Peggy Paige who would figure so prominently in the DPT story more than twenty years later.

The Devonshire Park Theatre did not open until 15 April, with a reprise of *The Wind and the Rain*. In the following week Jean Forbes-Robertson starred as *Mary Rose*. Perhaps even she was upstaged by Prime Minister Ramsay Macdonald, holidaying at the Grand Hotel.

Again the Park closed, and missed out on the Jubilee to celebrate King

George V's twenty-five years on the throne. It was the Pier Theatre that arranged for the radio broadcast of the King's speech to be relayed from the stage prior to the evening performance on Monday 6 May. Later the same evening at the Winter Garden, Roy Fox and his band led the Grand Jubilee Ball.

A cryptic notice appeared in the Eastbourne Gazette on 12 June announcing that the Devonshire Park Theatre would be closed until further notice. Uncertainty immediately arose as to the theatre's future, but one fact became clear in early July. Murray King announced that his current lease would expire at the end of the year and he would not be applying to renew it. The reporter writing in the Gazette dared wonder whether the Park would continue as a theatre at all or whether, 'like so many other similar buildings throughout the country, it is to be converted into a cinema.'

The chairman of the Devonshire Park and Baths Company, Charles Allix, attempted to allay fears by saying: 'The board are hopeful of carrying through negotiations which will result in the Devonshire Park being confirmed as a theatre.'

Murray King then plunged into what he described as his Farewell High Season Bookings. They began on 8 July with the play *The Dominant Sex*. They included *Sweet Aloes* on 2 September with 'the glamorous new star' Patricia Burke, the eighteen year-old daughter of Marie Burke. The last play in the High Season was *Family Affairs*, which starred Violet Vanbrugh.

Several touring productions followed, including a ballet week by Anton Dolin and Alicia Markova. There was also a special flying matinee of *Lady Precious Stream* featuring Esme Percy, Viola Tree and Mabel Constanduros.

Murray King then opened up in a frank interview on 18 September, in which he admitted his reasons for leaving.

'I am giving up because I think the building, under present conditions, is not up-to-date. There is still a public for the theatre proper, but with all the modern opposition the public naturally expect it at very reasonable prices, and this it is impossible to give when your building is tiny and your running expenses exorbitant. I daresay no-one realises the sums I have had to spend in that weather-beaten old Temple of the Drama. You must remember that I am only the lessee. I have been working out a few rough figures. Since I have been here I have paid over £43,000 in rent alone – enough, I should say, to buy the place over and over again. Rates, heating and insurance have cost me over £16,000 and indoor repairs over £10,000. These items are for the building alone, and do not include a penny towards the running of the entertainments. As I am, at the end of the year, faced with a bill of several thousands more in the way of dilapidations, I think it time I finished with the theatre before it finishes me.'

Speculation and gloom became rife in equal measure. Few letters had ever reached the correspondence columns of the local press about the playhouse but now they did. 'It looks as though we are about to lose our theatre,' bemoaned one correspondent. 'It is difficult to see how anyone else can make the Park Theatre a paying concern,' observed another.

There was talk in the November of a London syndicate negotiating for the theatre. A scheme had been advanced, allegedly, for the modernisation of the building. A rumour linked the names of well-known local people with the enterprise.

For the moment the only certainty was that Murray King would be leaving at the expiration of his lease on 31 December 1935, twenty-nine years after he and Charles Clark had taken on their first.

V

Uncertain Horizons

In the first months of 1936 darkness enveloped the Devonshire Park Theatre. Even the Christmas and New Year period saw the playhouse closed for the first time in thirty years. Murray King presented a pantomime as usual but it took place in the Winter Garden.

News was announced in April that two local businessmen had come to the rescue. Sir John Hammerton and Albert Donn formed a company called Eastbourne Theatre Limited and acquired a lease, to begin on 11 May.

A further redecoration programme went into full swing. New seating and carpeting were installed. The stage was refloored and a fireproof curtain provided. A switchboard and improved lighting effects were included. Dressing rooms were redecorated and hot and cold water plumbed into each. A larger canopy was placed over the entrance. The entire cost amounted to some £10,000.

Initial plans were announced for the summer. From 1 June there would be a five-week season under the title *Variety de Luxe* starring Renee Houston. It would be presented twice-nightly, at 6.35 and 8.50. Prices would range from 3/6d to 9d. For straight plays the equivalents would be 5/- to 1/-. The first three rows of the upper circle would be bookable at 1/6d. The Eastbourne Chronicle declared: 'Readers will join with us in wishing hearty success to the lessees of the theatre in their enterprise.'

In the Chronicle of 9 May 1936, the journalist G Gasson in his 'Stray Notes' column wrote the following.

'The reopening of the Devonshire Park Theatre on Monday next is an event of more than ordinary local interest. There is no denying that as an entertainment centre the theatre has been sorely missed especially by regular habituees who looked forward regularly and expectantly to the high-class dramatic fare that Mr Murray King never failed to provide.'

The latter reference appears to have been the sum total of tribute paid to Murray King. Other entertainment figures leaving the scene had been given considerable publicity and thanks for their work. For example, Captain H Amers who had conducted the municipal orchestra for fewer years than Murray King's tenure at the theatre was provided with a resounding send-off. Full page articles and pictures appeared about the man, and a benefit in his honour realised £205 which was handed to him. Murray King's departure apparently went largely unremarked. However, the old showman would leave an imprint on the opening night under the new management by a combination of his absence and good grace.

Monday 11 May 1936 was a grand occasion. A starry cast had been assembled to appear in *Short Story* by the young Robert Morley. Leading the company were Marie Tempest, Sybil Thorndike and A E Matthews. Among the supporting cast was Margaret Rutherford.

The new manager, Earnest J Borrow, made a speech declaring that Sir John Hammerton and Albert Donn had desired him to thank the large audience for crowding there 'in circumstances eloquent of good luck for their effort to revive the theatre-going habit in Eastbourne.'

Then came the moment of focus on the earlier incumbent. Earnest Borrow reported that Sir John had just received a telegram, despatched by radio from the middle of the Baltic Sea.

'Good luck and many happy returns – Murray King.'

Clearly the pantomime aficionado was on a vessel larger than his own yacht, the 'Cavallini'.

Following the reading of the telegram, Earnest Borrow said: 'That message would serve to show the audience the amicable relations that existed between the old regime and the new.'

The comment was greeted with applause.

The Eastbourne Chronicle reporter then recorded the following observation.

'They say you never realise the true value of a thing until you have lost it. It is true that we haven't lost the Park Theatre, but we have not seen a play here for over six months, and I have begun to understand more than ever before just what this cosy little place of entertainment means to me, and how keenly I should feel its loss if through lack of public support it ever closed its doors for good or for an extended period.'

Within a year, he would come close again to knowing what it could mean.

Meanwhile a busy summer and autumn ensued. Phyllis Neilson-Terry arrived once more to play *Mary Tudor*, presented by Ena G Lovell. A further ballet week from Anton Dolin and Alicia Markova was danced in July, presented by Vivian Van Damm.

Sybil Thorndike returned in the autumn with her own company at the same time as, in the north of England, the Jarrow crusade was beginning its march to London.

At Christmas the comments of the new management's opening night that relations with the old remained intact were found to be well placed when Murray King returned to produce his thirtieth pantomime, *Beauty and the Beast*.

Following which, Ena Lovell presented a new version of *Charley's Aunt* on 11 January 1937. Then the system collapsed for an undefined reason. The Devonshire Park Theatre went dark yet again for two months.

It was the same Ena G Lovell who would come to the rescue. On 6 March the Eastbourne Herald reported that Miss Lovell, a London theatrical manager, had taken out a sub-lease of the theatre from Eastbourne Theatre Limited 'for at least a year'. Miss Lovell was used to working at the seaside as she already had the lease on the Theatre Royal, Bognor. She had just dissolved her professional partnership with Barry O'Brien, who continued to present show tours until the 1960s. Two new managers were appointed consecutively in the course of the year.

Ena Lovell reopened the Devonshire Park Theatre on 15 March with a week of opera by the O'Mara Opera Company. Shortly after that Phyllis Dare starred in *And The Music Stopped*, which also featured Bernard Lee, eventually to be the first 'M' in many James Bond films.

The week of 10 May saw the country steeped in Coronation fever. Lucille Antone was appearing in *Dear Brutus* with Richard Hurndall. The curtain was held on the Wednesday, Coronation Day, so that the audience could hear the wireless broadcast by King George VI.

A new name presented the 1937 pantomime: the elegant entertainer, Randolph Sutton. *Jack and the Beanstalk* was on offer while Murray King competed with *Aladdin* at the Winter Garden.

One of the biggest achievements, both from theatrical and engineering points of view, was presented at the Devonshire Park Theatre on 1 August 1938 for a summer season. The show was Tom Arnold's musical on ice entitled *Switzerland.* A band of engineers moved into the theatre to install refrigerating plant, prior to the laying of the rink, all of which took place in the week before the opening.

The engineers worked night and day to fit into position four huge compressors, two brine tanks, and five miles of piping, which was laid into a special tank. When all was ready, refrigeration experts arrived to start the freezing process. The stage was transformed into a real ice rink with 1,200 square feet of ice, approximately two inches thick. Tom Arnold expressed his pride in the venture in an interview at the time.

'This is an entirely new angle of entertainment. From every point of view it has been a terrific job to make this show work. We have literally a dozen and one patents, and engineering experts of the world have consulted with me, and the result has been this marvellous quick freezing plant which has cost £14,000. The whole show is a blend of beauty, comedy and thrills. There are ballets and ensembles with all the performers on skates; burlesque items, and a sensational trick barrel jumping act. I have scoured the world for skaters of repute and ability. Altogether more than sixty skaters take part in the show.'

Furthermore, it was presented twice-nightly, at 6.20 and 8.50. It made the logistics of the Wembley Empire Circus of five years earlier seem like child's play.

After all the ice had been melted, Eastbourne audiences were introduced to the Brighton Repertory Company under the direction of W Forbes Russell. The repertory system was by now sprouting in theatres all over the land, part of the rationale being that communities would be able to have a group of actors they could get to know and enjoy seeing in a variety of roles. More will be discussed about the matter in later chapters.

From autumn 1938 to the spring of 1939, Forbes Russell presented a series of weekly plays while Ena G Lovell was in her third year as sub-lessee. The international storm clouds then brewing were to prelude a shorter rather than longer term of office for her.

The plays included *Jane Eyre*, *I Have Been Here Before* and *Private Lives*. The first presentation in Eastbourne of A A Milne's *Sarah Simple* was also presented under the Forbes Russell auspices.

The penultimate play in the Forbes Russell season was a production of Ibsen's *Ghosts*, for which the advertising literature clearly stated ADULTS ONLY. The last production was *Busman's Holiday*, among whose cast was the young Michael Balfour who went on to a successful post-war television career.

The Forbes Russell plays had often been directed by Brian Plunket Greene who had also taken acting parts in them. It was a company under the name of the Brian Plunket Greene Comedy Company which then took over from Monday 27 March 1939 with many of the same members continuing in residence. The first play was Noel Coward's *Hay Fever*.

Brian Plunket Greene was a nephew of Bronson Albery who owned, among several London theatres, the one known today by the family name in St Martin's Lane WC2 but which for many years was called the New Theatre.

Throughout the spring and summer of 1939 Plunket Greene continued to present weekly repertory. Frederick Lonsdale's *On Approval* was included in the programme along with Shaw's *Candida*. In *White Cargo*, Tondelayo was portrayed by Maud Long, one of the company's regulars. A comedy was given the FOR ADULTS ONLY label, a play entitled *The Greeks Had a Word For It*. It featured John Horsley who was to be a television name in years to come.

Various single weeks were given over to individual managements presenting plays that had just arrived from London or were about to go there. One example was Priestley's *When We Are Married* presented by Basil Dean. It must have been hilarious for it starred one of the grand old funny men of music hall, Robb Wilton.

It happened to be another impressario who put on the production in the week commencing Monday 28 August: an adaptation of Edgar Wallace's *Number Six*, presented by Prince Littler.

By the closing Saturday night, a lot of movement was taking place nationally. Throngs of children arrived at Eastbourne Station from London clutching gas masks. Eastbourne had been declared a safety zone. The following morning Neville Chamberlain addressed the nation at eleven o'clock. In common with all other theatres and cinemas in Eastbourne, the doors of the Devonshire Park Theatre were to remain padlocked for the time being as the country slid irretrievably into war for the second time in twenty-five years.

The phoney war syndrome soon took hold. A correspondent in the Eastbourne Herald berated young people for taking the view that the War was boring them. There would be plenty to do soon enough, prophesied the writer, and plenty of action in which to become involved.

One of the phoney war's results was that the Devonshire Park Theatre did not remain closed for long. Two months after the Declaration it reopened its doors, on 4 November.

A London producer who had already presented some work at the theatre, Leon M Lion, decided to move to the coast and take over at the DPT. He formed a company whose first production was Shaw's *You Never Can Tell.* He put on a different play each week and the last two weeks of the fateful year saw a variety of one-acters taken from Noel Coward's *Tonight at Eight*. Not all evenings saw performances but when they did they began at 7.45.

Mr Lion was clearly in charitable mood for the approaching Christmas as the Herald reported.

'A seasonable innovation announced by the management is that as from Monday 11 December all the seats in the Grand Circle will be available at the one price of half-a-crown (unreserved). Patrons may book in advance for an extra fee of sixpence. The teas served in the Grand Circle will also be cheaper.'

The bleakness of the first war-time winter continued apace. King George VI made his moving speech about the man who stood at the Gate of the Year, and on the first day of 1940, theatre struggled on bravely at Eastbourne. Leon M

Lion presented a play entitled *Number Seventeen* starring Nicholas Hannen. Exactly one week later, on Monday 8 January, rationing of butter, bacon and sugar began. A faint irony occurs in the title presented that night to Eastbourne audiences for the coming week: *Wisdom Teeth*. It was written by Noel Streatfeild, daughter of the Vicar of Eastbourne and subsequently Bishop of Lewes. It featured Donald Gray – destined to be a dinner-jacketed television announcer in the Fifties. He appeared with Renee Asherson (then Mrs Robert Donat), and a young John Arnatt, whose parents, Mr and Mrs Francis Arnatt lived at Friston, and John comes into the story again many years later.

Leon M Lion's plans changed suddenly – a common feature in wartime – and his final production opened on Monday 22 January. When George Bernard Shaw heard that he was presenting *The Millionairess* and that he was bringing an actress called Sarah Topping to play the title role, Shaw told Leon M Lion: 'She is the Millionairess!'

Miss Topping gained the local population's interest by recalling her encounter with Hitler four years earlier.

'It was just before the Olympic Games and I was visiting Berlin with a group of Japanese friends. We had lunch with the Fuhrer and we were lined up – a most objectionable sort of parading – for him to "inspect" us.

'I do not say it because of what has happened since, but I have never met anyone I disliked so much. He was working up for one of his fits of temper and there was a look in his eyes that made me think then that here was a man who was a complete lunatic. I took an intense dislike to him and I am afraid I showed it.'

W Forbes Russell returned to the Devonshire Park Theatre on 17 February 1940. He took over as sub-lessee, Ena Lovell having relinquished the post at the outbreak of war. One of Russell's assistants and members of Brighton Repertory Company, Gerald Alexander, took over as theatre manager.

For a while, during the continuance of the phoney war, entertainment in Eastbourne flourished. Competition was back. During the week beginning 18 March, *The School For Husbands* was being presented while down the road at the Royal Hippodrome a variety bill was being headed by Bransby Williams. The following week, on Easter Monday, at the Park J M Barrie's *Mary Rose* was presented and the public were advised beforehand, somewhat puzzlingly: 'A special production is being prepared with a due regard to the atmosphere of the Highlands.'

Yet between the two Mondays came the first sign in Eastbourne that the phoney war's days were numbered. Off the coast at Beachy Head, the ss Barnhill was bombed by the enemy on 20 March. It was the first local incident, and one involving loss of life; five crew members died.

Therein lay a particular coincidence. Over the Easter the vessel was slowly brought to Langney Point to be beached. Of necessity it came past the pier, whose own theatre was still functioning. Opening there that Easter Monday night was a production of Patrick Hamilton's *Gaslight*.

Picture its star getting ready in a pier dressing room to play Bella Manningham as the ss Barnhill is towed past. Could Sarah Churchill have had any notion that within months her father would be coming out of political obscurity to become, arguably, the century's greatest statesman?

On a prosaic level, war began to affect programme size. By the time of *The Constant Wife*, on 1 April, the programme was down from six or even eight pages to four. Yet competition still obtained on several levels. For example, in the week beginning 8 April, the Eastbourne Operatic and Dramatic Society was presenting two offerings, split midweek. *The Mikado* began the week and N C Hunter's *Grouse in June* completed it. On the Wednesday evening, meanwhile, in the Winter Garden, a 'Sensational Middleweight Contest' was billed, 'with Aircraftman Freddie Mills from RAF Bournemouth'.

By June 1940 the British Expeditionary Force had been evacuated from Dunkirk and it was thought that Germany was setting up an invasion plan. Aware of the mood the DPT management put out the sobering announcement on 8 June.

'Despite adverse circumstances, the Repertory Company intend to carry on and give local theatre patrons entertainment at popular prices.'

The announcement coincided with the first air raid warning (unfounded as it transpired) since the start of the War nine months earlier. The pier was closed down. Clarkson Rose's *Twinkle* company was hurriedly moved into the Winter Garden. The militia was about to impose a seafront curfew on Eastbourne.

W Forbes Russell soldiered on bravely but it was a losing battle, for the moment. A desperate move to boost audience numbers came in the special notice to patrons in the programme for *Cousin Muriel*, presented on 24 June.

'Everybody booking TWO SEATS for Saturday Night from Next Saturday onwards, will be given ONE FREE SEAT of the same value for the following week.'

On 1 July J B Priestley's new play prior to West End production, *The Long Mirror*, was presented and it starred Jean Forbes-Robertson and Andre Van Gysghem. It closed on Saturday 6 July. The following day, the first bombs hit Eastbourne, in the St Philip's Avenue area. Two people died. One day later, W Forbes Russell presented his final offering, the not-inappropriately titled *Yes And No*.

They lived to see another, and very long, day. The Forbes Russell Company eventually returned to the Palace Pier Theatre, Brighton until at least 1960, when Judy Cornwell recalls being a part of it.

So far from being a safety zone, as Eastbourne had been designated in 1939, the evacuation process went into reverse gear. On 15 July nearly 3,500 children left the town. The overall population was to reduce from sixty thousand to thirteen thousand people. 330 hotels and guest houses were to close to civilians and a ban on all visitors was not long in being imposed. The Battle of Britain was less than two months away.

The effect on the entertainment scene – in common with most places – was considerable. Of all its theatre shows, only Clarkson Rose's *Twinkle* survived to 7 September 1940. From the town's total of eight cinemas, only the Luxor and Picturedrome were still in operation by November.

The Devonshire Park Theatre was to experience the first of its dark periods of the War. It closed on 13 July for eighteen months. Although no records exist, it is possible that the playhouse started being used then as a Garrison Theatre with shows specially for troops stationed in the area. It is more likely, however, that the ENSA (later the Combined Services Entertainment) shows began at the Park at a later stage in the War.

Theatre lovers perked up at the announcement in the Eastbourne Herald on 1 November 1941.

'There is every prospect that the Devonshire Park Theatre will be reopened early in the new year. Negotiations are in progress for the presentation towards the end of January of Mr Clarkson Rose's pantomime, and this attractive event, it is hoped, will be followed by *Twinkle* for a short resident season.'

If Clarkie had been in some trepidation as to possible audience sizes, he would have been heartened at the news during the same month that the ban on visitors to the town was to be lifted.

A false sense of security was possibly setting in. The last bombing raid had taken place in early June 1941, in the St Leonard's Road area. Eastbourne was to be free of bombs for another eleven months. During that time, not only was the ban lifted but the Royal Hippodrome, which had also closed, reopened on 29 December with twice-nightly variety. For a while the Eastbourne Herald increased its size from eight to fourteen pages.

In the event, the DPT's commercial output in 1942 was meagre. It reopened on 19 January on the initiative of a name familiar to pre-war audiences. Bronson Albery's nephew, Brian Plunket Greene, had become an Army captain. He had been among those evacuated from Dunkirk and was now serving in Home Forces. He put on a twice-nightly programme for the 19 January week, starring Chang, the Chinese Illusionist. It closed abruptly on the Saturday night.

Clarkson Rose's pantomime did not materialise but he did bring back *Twinkle* for two weeks from 16 February. As ever his wife, Olive Fox, was very much part of the show. Also involved was Tommy Fields, Gracie's brother. At the piano was a lady who would become synonymous with Eastbourne entertainment, Dorothy Atlee.

For one week in March four plays were presented by the Eastbourne Wartime Committee. An appeal had gone forth to finance Eastbourne's own warship. The week's performances benefited the enterprise to the tune of £186.12.7d. The augmented orchestra was conducted by Jan Hurst, musical director of the Brighton Pavilion Orchestra.

Following the three false starts, the theatre closed again. The Hippodrome fared better with weekly variety and revue. The ban on visitors was re-imposed on 15 April 1942 and three weeks later the bombs were back. On 4 May St John's Church, Meads was destroyed as was the east wing of the Cavendish Hotel. Even the Royal Hippodrome gave up the ghost for the forseeable future. Once again only Eastbourne's cinemas – and many others besides the Luxor and Picturedrome gradually reopened – kept the 1943 entertainment scene afloat.

Evidence begins to emerge at the start of 1944 of productions arranged by the Department of National Service Entertainment (ENSA) at the Devonshire Park Theatre. Sadler's Wells Ballet gave three performances in January and then *Blithe Spirit* was presented on 11 April. An undated production of *She Follows Me About* was also given. This latter featured Joyce Heron, Robertson Hare, Catherine Lacey and Basil Radford. The following determined note appeared in the programme.

'Unrestrained coughing detracts from the enjoyment of the rest of the audience, and also makes the performance more difficult for the players. Will you do what you can to help? Thank you.'

It might have helped of course if they had not permitted smoking.

There was still no sign of the Devonshire Park Theatre opening on a commercial basis. The Royal Hippodrome set the pace on Bank Holiday, 7 August, perhaps somewhat nervously as 1944 was the year of the doodlebugs. But exactly one week later the final flying bomb attack on Eastbourne was made, exploding near Holywell.

Hope was in the air. D-Day had occurred two months earlier and advances were being made across occupied Europe. Newspapers were full of discussion about post-war planning. The Eastbourne Herald caught the mood, reporting debates on future housing and education. On 2 September it carried an interview with the man who had been in charge of the Devonshire Park Theatre for most of the century's first half.

In his own dreams of post-war entertainment, Murray King wanted to see a clean sweep made of anything that had 'the least taint of suggestiveness on the stage.' He was 'jealous of the good name of the theatre' and he would be 'pained if anything happened to besmirch it'. The theatre provided the natural setting 'for romance, for chivalry, for gallantry, for clean comedy and high tragedy. May it never fail in that function.'

By September 1944, much of Eastbourne's beach was reopened and people could stroll along the seafront again, having been prevented from doing so for four years. The Benson Repertory Company moved into the Royal Hippodrome on 25 September, to be followed in November by the Earl Armstrong Company. Central Bandstand concerts returned in December, but still no sign of the DPT reopening.

One effect of the lack of the arts on account of war was highlighted in the 'Young Eastbourne' weekly column of the Herald by 'Juvens' on 28 October.

'Youth discussion at the YMCA showed that because of war, many 16/17 year-olds had never been to a theatre to see a play. One wishes that every youth club in Eastbourne would introduce its members to at least one good straight play in the professional theatre before the winter is over.'

The early months of 1945 saw increased activity as it became ever clearer that the struggle for peace was coming to an end. At least two further productions for armed services personnel took place. These were now under the auspices of Combined Services Entertainment. Agatha Christie's *Ten Little Niggers* was presented on 5 January with Edgar K Bruce as William Blore. Peggy Forbes-Robertson and Anna Turner were among those to appear in *Scandal at Barchester* on 22 March. Occasional concerts returned to the Winter Garden. The London Symphony Orchestra made appearances under their conductor, Basil Cameron. In the spring the Redoubt Music Gardens reopened, as did some of the 330 hotels and guest houses. In common with most towns all over Britain, Eastbourne let joy be unconfined with speeches and street parties on VE Day in May.

Much remained to be done. War still raged in the Far East, involving many thousands of allied forces. A massive rebuilding programme concentrated minds. A few days after the General Election was held, the Devonshire Park Theatre reopened, on Monday 30 July.

With the collective mind preoccupied, the opening took place with little fanfare. The theatre was now controlled by Charles W Bell, the new holder of a sub-lease from Eastbourne Theatre Limited. The productions were in the hands of Barry O'Brien for a while, beginning with *Is Your Honeymoon Really Necessary?*

The following week saw Terence Rattigan's *Flare Path* and the third play was *Pink String and Sealing Wax*. This Roland Pertwee comedy featured Nancy Roberts. Ten years later Miss Roberts would achieve national fame as the crotchety old Gran of twelve year-old Christopher Beeny in television's *The Grove Family*, written by Michael Pertwee, Roland's son. The assistant stage manager was John Forbes-Robertson.

The top price stalls seat was 6/-d (30p) and owing to paper shortage, programme size was reduced to four pages.

The Devonshire Park Theatre now made up for lost time. Once more a different play was featured each week. 1 October saw a production of *The Lovely Lady* starring someone befitting the description. Chili Bouchier had foregone the chance of a Hollywood career in the Thirties to return to Britain and embark on a lifetime's work in the theatre.

Later in the month Sonia Dresdel starred in *Green Laughter* with Anthony Hawtrey, and the following week a touring production of A Doll's House arrived at Compton Street. Angela Baddeley played the lead, some thirty years before achieving popular recognition as Mrs Bridges in *Upstairs, Downstairs*. Her leading man was John Stuart and one of the children was played by Joyce Blair.

A new comedy, *Fit For Heroes*, by Harold Brooke and Kay Bannerman came to the theatre on 12 November. It starred Dame Irene Vanbrugh and among the cast were Ursula Howells and Olaf Pooley. Also featured was Lois Maxwell, still seventeen years away from becoming Miss Moneypenny in *Dr No* and a run of James Bond sequels. The stage staff are of equal interest. The ASM was Gwen Cherrell and the stage manager was a nineteen year-old June Whitfield.

Having been presented with a photocopy of the November 1945 programme, and asked for confirmation that she stage managed *Fit For Heroes*, Miss Whitfield wrote back as follows.

'Yes, indeed 'twas I, and it was part of a tour though not a long one. We were supposed to end up at the Whitehall Theatre in 1946 but were pipped at the post by Brian Rix.

'Dame Irene was delightful: I always wanted to curtsey when we met – she had such dignity. I had worked with her before, in *Appointment With Fear*, assistant stage managing and playing a small part. I don't really remember how Gwen and I came to stage manage *Fit For Heroes* but once the stage crew realised we knew what we were doing (bluffing our way), they seemed to accept the situation'.

WEEK COMMENCING MONDAY, 19th NOVEMBER, 1945

ANTHONY AND MARJORY HAWTREY present

FIT FOR HEROES

A Farcical Comedy by HAROLD BROOKE and KAY BANNERMAN

Characters in order of their appearance:

Mr. Briggs, an Estate Agent	ARTHUR GOULLET	Horace Barnett ..	OLAF POOLEY
Lady Wimpole	IRENE VANBRUGH	Major the Hon. George Wimpole, D.S.O., M.C.	HUMPHREY MORTON
Lord Wimpole	RAYMOND LOVELL		
James, the Butler ..	EDGAR NORFOLK	Lieut. Mary Hobart, U.S. Army	LOIS MAXWELL
The Hon. Elizabeth Wimpole	URSULA HOWELLS		

The Play directed by HENRY KENDALL

The action of the Play takes place in a Portal House in Kent. Time—The Present

ACT I SCENE 1 An afternoon
SCENE 2 A fortnight later, after tea
ACT II The following morning
ACT III The same afternoon

The Scene designed by Marigold Taylor, built by Alfred Harris and painted by Mary Purvis. The Act Drop designed and painted by Marigold Taylor. Furniture by the Old Times Furnishing Co. Properties by Robinson Bros. Electrical Properties by Strand Electric. Costumes by Samuels. Stuffed birds by Messrs. Gerrards. The billiards table and cues kindly lent by Messrs. Riley. Cigarettes by Abdulla.

Business Manager ..	Laurence Atteridge	Stage Manager	June Whitfield
Asst. Stage Manager ..	Gwen Cherrell	Press Representative	William Wordsworth

For Anthony and Marjory Hawtrey

Entr'acte Music by the Theatre Trio. Leader LUCIEN MOTYLINSKI

The last year of the Second World War ended on a high note in Eastbourne. At the Royal Hippodrome Theatre the prime minister of mirth, Sir George Robey appeared in an offering entitled *Christmas Pie*. At the Devonshire Park Theatre, the man who had commanded the theatre for many years from the early 1900s returned for what was billed as a Farewell Appearance. The Eastbourne Herald offered the glad tidings on 22 December 1945.

'One thing that Eastbourne missed during wartime Christmases was the annual pantomime at the Devonshire Park Theatre, produced by that expert in these matters, Murray King. Well, the War has ended, peace has come, and this experienced entrepreneur once more shoots up through a trap-door in the stage and exclaims merrily (we had almost said Murrayly): "Here we are again – this time with *Mother Goose*." It will indeed be like old times to see this popular comedian playing the dame again.'

PROGRAMME

MURRAY KING

AND HIS

FAREWELL CHRISTMAS PANTOMIME

"MOTHER GOOSE"

Book by Hickory Wood. Music composed, selected and arranged by Fred Seymour, L.R.A.M.

The whole Pantomime designed, produced and arranged by Murray King and Edgar Sawyer

Characters

Belsen (A Demon) .. .. .. LOUIS JENART

Saccharina (A Fairy) .. .. JOSEPHINE WARD

The Squire. Just returned home, after keeping up Britain's Morale, for six years, at Llundudno ; gets everything he wants from local tradesmen .. CLIFFORD WARREN

Mother Goose (Who has stayed put, gets the bird) .. .. MURRAY KING

Katie (The Bird) .. .. .. GEORGE CLARK

Giles (Her elder son) .. .. EDGAR SAWYER

Colin (Her younger ditto) .. .. HAZEL GAY

Tina (Poor little rich girl) .. .. LESLEY DARELL

The Duchess of Crumbles .. .. .. ROSA REY

Claude Laval (A Highwayman) .. VIVIAN MICHAELS

Horace (A County Buck) .. .. FRANK RAYMOND

Father Christmas .. .. .. JOHN HARCOURT

CATALOGUE OF THE POULTRY FARM

Pen 1 .. .. A Gloomy Gorge

Pen 2 .. .. The Village of Milldyke (East Coast)

Pen 3 .. .. The Squire's Parlour

Pen 4 .. .. The Fish Queue

Pen 5 .. .. .. Ballroom of The Chateau Chimmy

Pen 6 .. .. A Village Lane

Pen 7 .. .. Outside the Wishing Well

Pen 8 "Transformation Scene " The Valley of Memories."
Danielova Ballet. Principal Dancer, Marianne.
Marianova Dancers. Renee Dymott, The Spirit of Youth

Interval

Pen 9 .. .. Ye Olde Dutch Garden

Pen 10 .. .. Outside the Wee Kirk

Pen 11 .. .. The Wishing Gate

Pen 12 .. .. Mother Goose's Boudoir
Josephine and Jenart. The B.B.C. Soprano and Belgium's Premier Tenor

Pen 13 .. .. Ye Tabs

Pen 14 .. .. .. Grove in the Palace of Palms
The Six Mighty Atoms

Several old favourite scenes will be included by request.

Scenery by Berre and Browne. Built by James Greatorex.
Choreography by Gwenda Tallent.
Dresses by Charles H. Fox Ltd. and Bevan Lorimer.
Murray King's Dresses by Madame Pauline Herbert.

Musical Director .. For Murray King — Fred Seymour, L.R.A.M.
Stage Director .. Frank Raymond
Stage Manager .. James Greatorex
Wardrobe Mistress Gladys Croft

Licensee and General Manager .. Charles W. Bell
Stage Manager .. .. Dick Selby
Electrician .. .. William Trusler
Resident Musical Director .. .. Lucien Motylinski

For Charles W. Bell and T. L. Powys Keck

December 1945

VI

A Busy Peace

The Devonshire Park Theatre embarked on its first full year in peace time since 1939 and the first production centred decisively on the theme of peace. Italia Conti appeared in and directed *Where The Rainbow Ends*, described as 'the Patriotic Play of British ideals which has run for over thirty-five years in London'. Written by Clifford Mills and John Ramsey, its music was by Roger Quilter.

Italia Conti was coming to the end of her life at the time. The stage school she founded and which bears her name continues in London. She used many of her youngsters for the various productions of *Where The Rainbow Ends*, including a boy called Peter Byrne.

Local audiences had a second bite of pantomime in January 1946 when Clarkson Rose brought in his production of *Aladdin* which had just been staged at the White Rock Pavilion, Hastings.

Following on was a play entitled *So Brief The Spring*. Its leading players were Robert Newton and Barbara Mullen. Mr Newton did not have to travel far as his home was then Tickeridge Mill, Uckfield, which was eventually to be the last home of Vivien Leigh.

Murray King's *Mother Goose* had already been staged but the Eastbourne Herald gave the news that as so many people had been turned away from the fortnight's run at Christmas, Charles W Bell had arranged for its return of a further week at the end of January.

It was in the same month that the question of Sunday opening of Eastbourne cinemas was finally settled. After the War had ended, a move had been made to revert to Sunday closure. The Town Council decided to hold a local referendum. The result was nearly eleven thousand in favour of continued opening, and fewer than three thousand against.

Roy Limbert's Malvern Company took over for six weeks at the DPT beginning in late February, presenting among others, *This Happy Breed*, *Blithe Spirit*, and *Pygmalion*.

At the same time the local press was concerned about the banana shortage. As many young people had never seen one, the Herald ran a series of pictures illustrating how to eat the particular fruit and included advice on what not to do with the skin in order to avoid accidents!

During one particular week in March 1946, a revue entitled *Ripples of Mirth* was staged at the Royal Hippodrome Theatre. Its star, described as the 'Rarebit of Fun' was Bunny Baron, whose future wife, Lisa, would become in the early 1990s the manager of the Devonshire Park Theatre.

A certain amount of excitement was stirred in the town during the week in April that the DPT hosted the Peter Dearing production, *Dear Evelyn*, featuring Adrianne Allen, Gladys Henson and Charles Lefaux. A film company led by Sidney and Muriel Box was creating action scenes at the pier for their production of *Girl in a Million* with Hugh Williams and Joan Greenwood.

A further local link occurred during the week of 20 May. While Terence de Marney was appearing in *Dear Murderer* at the Park, the twice-nightly variety bill at the Royal Hippodrome included 'the Zyli-Fool', Sid Plummer. A few decades later, his son and daughter-in-law, Tommy Wallis and Beryl, were to take up residence in Eastbourne as well as appearing regularly in the town themselves, billed as The Plummers.

Phyllis Neilson-Terry made one of her now frequent appearances in June together with Heron Carvic who also wrote the play being presented, *The Widow at 40.* On the Sunday evening preceding their opening, Tommy Handley appeared at the Winter Garden. He would have had ample material based on food shortages. The Eastbourne Herald was busy explaining the lack of potatoes and produced headlines such as 'Apples may arrive at any time', and 'More tomatoes expected next week.'

A play called *Frieda* appeared in July and told of a British soldier serving in Germany in the War who brings home a German wife. The play clearly touched on the danger of making generalisations about nations. The Eastbourne Herald sympathised with the play's message. Given that the War in Europe had ended only a year before, it must have been an encouraging, perhaps even brave, exercise. Taking the title role was an actress called Annabelle Maule. Two years later her father, Donovan, made his mark with the theatre in his own name in Nairobi, Kenya, which was to run successfully for nearly forty years.

While Diana Churchill appeared in *Soldier's Wife* in the second week of July 1946, Eric Winstone was playing a week of dances at the Winter Garden. He took on three young songstresses for the vocals: the Beverley Sisters.

The Shop at Sly Corner played a week in August with Bransby Williams taking the lead. A young Kevin Sheldon was also in the cast. Eight years later he was producing and directing one of television's first families, *The Appleyards*. The present writer still recalls making a visit as a thirteen year-old to Studio E at Lime Grove and finding Phil Tate and his orchestra in one half of the studio rehearsing for their live show at five o'clock, while the Appleyards were in the other half where they would follow on half an hour later.

Clarkson Rose brought *Twinkle* back home for a three-week run in September. The following month the Irish Players arrived to perform *The*

Whiteheaded Boy. One of their number was Wilfred Brambell. A play called *Caste*, presented in November, featured Bill Rowbotham, before he changed his name to Bill Owen. A misprint also announced a young actress called Brenda Luce; her surname was Bruce.

In late October 1946, Anthony Hawtrey brought a production of *Jane Eyre* to Eastbourne, in which he played Mr Rochester, and Mary Mackenzie took the title role. The week provided a touching moment when it marked the first theatre visit by Miss Constance Levett of Arlington at the age of 48. Wheelchair-bound since childhood, she was staying at All Saints' Hospital for a three-week rest, by courtesy of the Sussex Cripples Association.

Fiercely independent, Miss Levett claimed she 'always did for herself' and had been an active member of her local Women's Institute for eighteen years. Her one regret had been that as soon as her childhood illness had been diagnosed, she had been taken away from school, never to complete her education. The Eastbourne Herald's sub headline of the story summed up the mood and language of the times: 'Cripple who does housework in wheelchair.'

25 November and week saw Bernard Delfont's presentation of *Duet For Two Hands* by Mary Hayley Bell. It featured Maureen Pook (later Pryor) and Margot Boyd, destined eventually for the role of Mrs Antrobus in *The Archers*. In the same week the film for which location shooting had taken place in Eastbourne several months earlier, *Girl in a Million*, was playing to packed houses at the Picturedrome.

Returning to production after six years of war-time absence, the Eastbourne Operatic and Dramatic Society presented *Yeomen of the Guard* and *My Lady's Dress* on 2 December 1946. The cast included Stephen Brewer, whose family contributed an inestimable amount to the town's dramatic and musical life, and would continue to do so for years to come. His son, Mark Brewer, instigated the Tivoli Performing Arts Centre and Stephen himself continues to direct for EODS.

Cinderella went to the ball in a golden coach from 26 December by courtesy of Murray King, of whom the Eastbourne Herald observed:

'He has been gravely announcing it as his 35th farewell pantomime. But we know our Murray. He will have his little joke.'

The winter of 1947 was the worst on record. During the run of the pantomime, alarm was raised by hoteliers in the face of Energy Minister Shinwell's demands for fuel cuts. The Roy Limbert Malvern Company came back to play for another six weeks, during which further appeals were made to cut down on electricity, this time from the Prime Minister, Clement Attlee. The Young Vic arrived to perform *The King's Stag*, directed by George Devine. The company built scenery in the theatre by candlelight to the sound of a raging blizzard outside.

As Eastbourne started to thaw out, Cathleen Nesbitt arrived in March to star in *Message For Margaret*. A further spring tonic followed in April. A com-

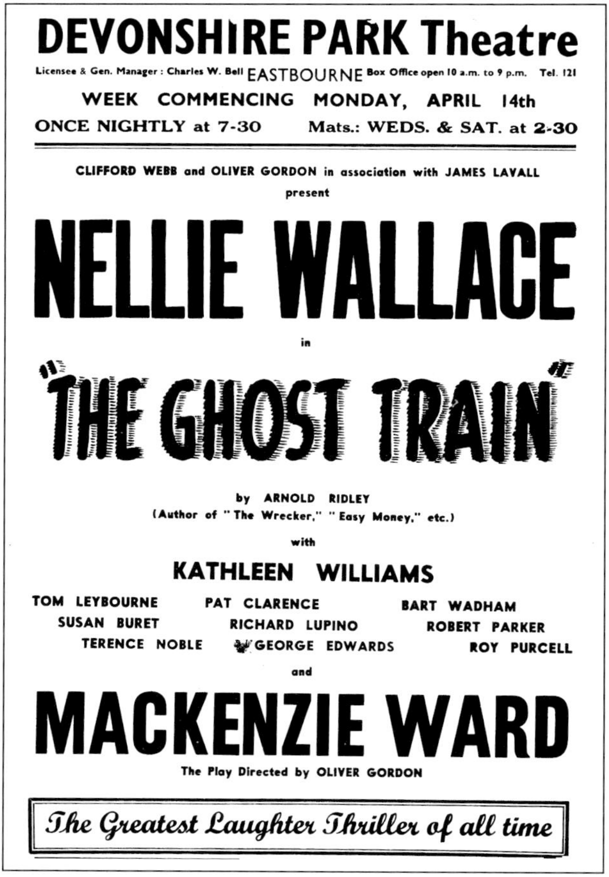

April 1947

pany came to play a week's run of Arnold Ridley's *The Ghost Train.* It was led by the great music-hall star, Nellie Wallace, making a rare excursion into 'legit' theatre.

Much of Miss Wallace's notable career had been spent at the London Palladium. As well as appearing on the opening night bill of the world-famous variety theatre, she played long runs in the revues *Whirl of the World* and *Sky High* in the 1920s. It was to prove her last workplace too. Eighteen months after her appearance at the Devonshire Park Theatre, Nellie Wallace was selected yet again to appear in the Royal Variety Performance. She completed her act and as she came offstage that November night in 1948, she collapsed with heart trouble and died a few days later.

While Sean O'Casey's *Oak Leaves and Lavender* was playing a week in May 1947 – and featuring the soubrette, Sheila Sim – local press and public were highly exercised by increasing traffic congestion in Terminus Road. To ease the growing problem a link road was proposed via Tideswell Road to connect at the junction of Langney and Terminus Roads.

Another social situation bubbled at the same time: the housing shortage. Later in May the Eastbourne Herald's wide headline roared the solution: BIG HOUSES IN MEADS FOR WORKING CLASS FAMILIES.

At the time, the Firth Shephard Company was presenting *Arsenic and Old Lace* at the Devonshire Park Theatre. The juvenile role was taken by Nicholas Parsons. An equally young Anton Rodgers featured at the end of the month in a production of *Great Expectations,* in which Bransby Williams played Magwitch.

Barry O'Brien put on a short season in early summer. It included *The Lady From Edinburgh* with Raymond Francis, by then a local family man, steadily making progress in his career. On 22 June, the night before the play began, Richard Tauber appeared at the Winter Garden, to be followed two weeks later by the erstwhile portrayer of the title role in Chaplin's *The Kid*, Jackie Coogan.

1947 was the year of the Fleming Report into independent schools. It was advocated that such schools be opened up to children of less financially fortunate families. Warren Chetham-Strode wrote of the situation in *The Guinea Pig*. Playing the boy Read, the title role, in the July production at the DPT was Oscar Quitak.

Twinkle returned for another summer season, during which technology concerning the small screen continued to struggle. Efforts had been made to deliver images of the town to the nation. A BBC technician was reported as saying that there were difficulties enough in getting television pictures transmitted from Southend which was only half the distance from London. Given the 'obstacle' of the South Downs, it was impossible to contemplate success as far as Eastbourne was concerned. The technician went on to say: 'But the idea hasn't been spiked.'

A company new to the town arrived in late September for a six-week season. The Embassy Theatre Company's productions included *Blithe Spirit*, *Power Without Glory*, and *Laura*. Among the youthful company members were Patrick Cargill, Lyndon Brook and Gwendoline Watford. Midway through the season the Herald announced: 'Another charming newcomer to the company is Leslie Phillips.'

Phyllis Dixey was an artist known for her scantily-clad appearances or, as the Eastbourne Gazette expressed it, 'a revue star of a most self-revealing character'. However, in 1947 she embarked on a more serious project. She herself presented a new play entitled *Marry Or Burn* and brought it to the Devonshire Park Theatre on 13 November.

Concerned with a problem of the post-war world, its writer, Charlotte Francis, posed the question whether life was worth living in the reality of the new Atomic age. It was a theme common to much writing of the time. Even Noel Langley's wafer-thin comedy, *Little Lambs Eat Ivy*, touched on it.

Marry Or Burn centred upon a demobbed young commando, newly returned from what he had seen as the folly of war. Life had little to offer with no point in striving when at any moment mankind might be blown to pieces.

Anthony Eustrel was the commando and Phyllis Dixey played 'an eminently logical-minded and efficient young woman' who came along to convince him life was worth living after all. It was a part that reportedly gave Miss Dixey's acting ability full scope for she had scenes of comedy, strength and tenderness.

Having established the play's lofty credentials, the Eastbourne Gazette went on to report with the journalistic equivalent of a straight face: 'Miss Phyllis Dixey also plays the part of a statue so her admirers in that line are also catered for'.

It seemed that Christmas 1946 truly had seen Murray King's 'Farewell Pantomime', for now Rudolph's reins were in the hands of Clarkson Rose who presented *Red Riding Hood* for the 1947 season. At the same time, in ration-living Britain, the Brighton Butchers' Association put out the dismal news: 'No pork this Christmas.'

1948 began with two short repertory seasons. The Philip Barrett Company took up residence for eight weeks followed by a second run from the Embassy Theatre Company. Among the latter's contingent were added Jill Bennett and Richard Bebb (who married Gwen Watford).

In April H J Barlow brought *Worm's Eye View* – then in its third year at the Whitehall Theatre – to Eastbourne. At the same time Winston Churchill was given the Freedom of the town, nearly half a century after he had delivered his Boer War lecture at the Devonshire Park Theatre.

A Sunday evening in May at the Winter Garden saw Vic Oliver conducting the British Concert Orchestra. Performing second on the bill was 'A New Sensational twelve year-old Soprano: Julie Andrews.'

7 June and week brought Edgar K Bruce to the Park to star in *Pick Up Girl*. The Eastbourne Herald of two days earlier delivered a health warning.

'The play deals with the momentous subject of juvenile delinquency. This is a play which is a true and moving document, frank and outspoken, blinking nothing *(sic)*, but treating a great human problem with a simple, heartfelt sincerity. It is not a stunt; it is a serious contribution to social welfare through the medium of the drama.

The following week was a busy one in Eastbourne. The Pier Theatre opened its *Star Wagon* summer season, which had established itself following the end of the War but there was now a change of star. Taking the place of Dan Leno Jnr was Sandy Powell who, together with his wife, Kay White, was to remain in residence for most of the next twenty summers. Clarkson Rose returned to the Devonshire Park Theatre for another short season of *Twinkle*.

While it was playing, the Winter Garden hosted the annual conference of the Urban District Councils Association. On Wednesday 23 June it was addressed by the Minister of Health, Aneurin Bevan, who was to launch the National Health Service less than a fortnight later. On this occasion, however, his subject was the Local Government Act which was being coaxed through Parliament.

In a brief section of his speech, Nye Bevan quoted one of the Act's most important provisions: that which enabled local authorities to spend up to a six-penny rate a year on entertainments, recreations and arts of various kinds.

Pleading for diversified cultural amenities, Mr Bevan said he believed it was because of cultural starvation that young people went to the cinema 'week after week'. This was his answer to people who asked why local authorities should enter the commercial field.

'The pursuit of money in entertainment has meant deterioration in the cultural standards of the community.'

Clarkson Rose was livid. He wrote to the Herald from his Granville Road home the following week.

'Are we to understand that if local authorities run theatres and entertainments, the pursuit of money is ruled out? I am not against local authorities running theatres but there can be no gainsaying the fact that the commercial theatre does this job far better.

'Does Aneurin Bevan really believe that local authorities could compare with the pioneers like Irving, Tree, Wyndham, Edwardes and D'Oyle Carte, or their present-day counterparts such as Cochran, Tennent, the Littlers, Hylton, Wolfit and Olivier?

'All these managements have pursued money; sometimes made it, sometimes lost it. They stand or fall by their knowledge, and when they fall, it isn't the ratepayer that has to pay the bill.

'In our own town the Devonshire Park Theatre is a commercial theatre, it has had its vicissitudes, but it has a reputation in our profession far beyond the confines of Eastbourne. It has built its reputation under the management of men who knew their craft. Its cultural contribution to the social life of Eastbourne needs no emphasis from me. I am convinced that not one of its patrons would like to see it run by a local authority. Please leave the theatre alone, Mr Bevan.'

If 'Clarkie' had entertained an inkling of the changing scene during the course of the following two or three decades, he would clearly have had a seizure.

For a week in July came *Tuppence Coloured* direct from the Globe Theatre, Shaftesbury Avenue (now the Gielgud). Presented by Laurier Lister, the revue starred Joyce Grenfell, Elizabeth Welch and Max Adrian.

That summer saw comedians old and new at the Royal Hippodrome. The celebrated Max Miller appeared for a week in August and, taking the top spot two months later, billed as 'the new young comedian', was Norman Wisdom.

The late Forties was still a time of scant competition from television. Complaining of amateur radio enthusiasts breaking into his television signal,

Mr N Facey of 23 Penhale Road protested in the correspondence column of the Eastbourne Herald.

'Television programming is short: one hour in the afternoon and one and a half hours at night, namely 3 to 4pm and 8.30 to 10.00pm. Surely the radio hams can afford to let us have these two short periods free from these kaleidescopic forms and noise which spoil an otherwise very pleasant form of entertainment.'

In the same week of the hot summer of 1948 the Dental Estimates Board moved into Temple Grove and the Herald could not resist the headline: 'Eastbourne is nation's mouthpiece.'

Following the summer swell of variety and revue, autumn brought the theatrical scene back to harsh reality with the arrival of *No Trees In The Street*, clearly billed 'For Adults Only'. Its author was a young and rising playwright of the Left, Ted Willis. He had done much work at the Unity Theatre in north London and was commenting increasingly on London life. By October 1948 he was busy with his creation of PC George Dixon, to be introduced within a year or so in the film *The Blue Lamp*. Even though George was to be killed off in the first twenty minutes by the young thug played by Dirk Bogarde, Jack Warner's character was to be resurrected to stay in the nation's heart until some thirty years later.

No Trees In The Street presented Ted Willis' picture of a London he knew vividly, and the somewhat patronising review in the Eastbourne Herald clearly assumes many of its readers had no such knowledge.

'A Slice of Raw Life is how the dramatic critic of the London 'Star' described *No Trees In The Street*, the new drama by Ted Willis which is due to play at the Devonshire Park Theatre next week. And indeed this is putting it mildly.

'The action is set in a present-day slum in the East End of London. Here we are introduced to all the sordid elements that go to make up life in that quarter – the spivs, the gangs, the drunkards.

'From the very moment the curtain rises, the audience is gripped, for here is the too-familiar story of juvenile delinquency with tragic sequels – the conditions under which lads are induced to adopt criminal tendencies with the inevitable result of complete disregard for the upholders of the law; and where young girls sink to the pitiful depths that already enfold their mothers.

'Cockney wit is prevalent throughout the play, and whilst the main theme will jerk the onlooker into shocked reality, there are many laughs.

'A brilliant cast of young actors and actresses are interpreting *No Trees In The Street* and the entire presentation is direct from the St James' Theatre, London.'

Eastbourne returned to safer territory with the late autumn production of *Random Harvest*. It starred a new British film husband and wife team, Hazel Court and Dermot Walsh. A week in December gave audiences the chance to see a legendary Gaiety Girl. The play was entitled *What Lies Beyond*, and portraying The Medium was Ruby Miller

Christmas arrived to find Clarkson Rose at the helm again, presenting *The Sleeping Beauty*. At the Royal Hippodrome for the same season a group of ex-servicemen from wartime entertainment put on *Forces Showboat*. The Herald critic was moved to comment: 'The surprise turn of the show is that of Harry Secombe.'

New year 1949 brought to the Devonshire Park Theatre Shaw's *Mrs Warren's Profession*. The Herald was glad to find itself keeping pace by announcing: 'Times have changed since the days when matters connected with sex were taboo.'

Perhaps the management was attempting to get the theatre-goers acclimatised for what was in store. On 22 April Eastbourne audiences were presented for the first time with *The Glass Menagerie* by Tennessee Williams. Starring as the terrifying mother was the American actress who had settled in Britain, Bessie Love. The Herald declared: 'Nothing quite like it has ever before been seen in England.'

Voice of the Turtle was the first play to be presented by Barry Morse as actor/manager. He brought it to the Park on 7 May 1949, co-starring with Nova Pilbeam. Mr Morse went on to find fame in Hollywood as Inspector Gerrard forever hounding David Jansen's *The Fugitive*. His son, Hayward Morse, would in years to come appear in summer season for Newpalm Productions.

The week beginning 6 June provided residents and visitors with a diverse choice. At the Park they could see Catherine Lacey, Beatrice Varley and Raymond Huntley in *The Late Edwina Black*. Making one of many return visits to the Royal Hippodrome for twice-nightly variety were Elsie and Doris Waters. Appearing at the Winter Garden was a member of a Hollywood institution, Chico Marx.

Following Clarkson Rose's *Twinkle* season came Harry Welchman in *Uncle Charley*, presented in July. Alongside the advertisement for the play was another for the furniture store, Perrings. They were able to offer a 'Single bedstead set, including headboard' for £8.19.6d.

At the beginning of August Barry O'Brien presented a short season including *The Paragon* and *Edward, My Son*. At the same time the Grand Hotel was offering dinner dances on Saturdays – evening dress requested – for 9/6d. The dance only would cost takers 5/- (25p).

At the Park Mary Jerrold came to take the title role in *Miss Mabel*. Playing the gardener was Arthur Lowe. In the same September week, the bill at the Royal Hippodrome featured Binnie Hale, Joe Church and the 'Housewives' Choice', George Elrick.

An offer from British Railways appeared in the Eastbourne Herald as follows.

'Join the Theatre Special to see Gracie Fields at the London Palladium,

Wednesday 5 October. Includes rail fare, tea and supper on the train, coach to and from the theatre, ticket for the show and a short sight-seeing drive through London. 3.39pm from Eastbourne, 10.15pm return from Victoria. 32/- (£1.60)'

October 15 saw the opening night at the Devonshire Park Theatre of a new play with music entitled *Lisette* by Douglas Sargent. It starred the eighteen year-old Diana Dors. Said the Herald:

'Many cinema-goers will welcome an opportunity to see this young, blonde and hazel-eyed actress in person.'

Later the same month a production was mounted at the Winter Garden for two performances by Eastbourne Young Conservatives. It was entitled *Third Time Lucky,* and the reviewer said of a future mayor: 'Aubrey Vickers did well as the scoundrel, Crowther.'

Before Clarkson Rose presented his third consecutive pantomime, *Babes in the Wood*, on Christmas Eve 1949, three autumn productions introduced audiences to people who would become national figures in the ensuing years. There was, for instance, Edna Dore who appeared in Emlyn Williams' *A Murder Has Been Arranged*, presented by Cambrian Productions. Four decades later Miss Dore would play Frank Butcher's mother in *EastEnders* before returning to Eastbourne for the filmed television series, *Westbeach.* Terence Rattigan's *Love In Idleness* featured Tom Fleming, who would take over from Richard Dimbleby in providing commentary for national occasions. Then there was Ruth Dunning who appeared in *Tobacco Road* only five years before becoming known as the matriarchal Mrs Grove in *The Grove Family.*

Tobacco Road is worthy of closer inspection. It was one of those plays that carried with it sufficient risk to cause surprise at its presentation in Eastbourne. Written by Jack Kirkland, *Tobacco Road* was adapted from Erskine Caldwell's novel. It had been banned for twelve years and in November 1949 the publicity for it at the Devonshire Park Theatre included the observation: 'The Management do not recommend this play as suitable for young people.'

The play had finally been passed by the Lord Chamberlain on assurance from the American producer, Robert Henderson, that its staging would be treated 'authentically and with sincerity'. Reported the Eastbourne Herald:

'The presentation shocked America, disgusted and confounded the critics, yet went on to become the world's longest theatrical run over a period of ten years on Broadway. It started six weeks ago in London with Mervyn Johns and Thora Hird.'

From a distance of almost fifty years, it is perhaps not so much a question of being surprised that a play such as *Tobacco Road* could cause such a furore. But it is surely awesome to countenance the notion of Dame Thora being mixed up in it.

VII

Which Way Now?

The mid-century point coincided with a watershed reached at the Devonshire Park Theatre. Around the country it was the heyday of the repertory companies. By the mid-Fifties, books were written about the system and radio and television programmes were devoted to their work. The process had often been a feature, albeit a chequered one, at the Royal Hippodrome since the 1930s, and the post-war years had re-established twice-nightly variety at the Seaside Road theatre. But by the start of 1950, Harry Hanson's Court Players were installed in the Hippodrome.

At the Devonshire Park Theatre the situation had been different. There had certainly been short seasons of rep going back as far as Alfred Wareing's days in 1916. But they had never lasted more than six weeks at most with the exception of the Forbes Russell Company in the late Thirties. Now, at the start of 1950, it was as though sub-lessee Charles W Bell was taking a deep breath and plunging into the repertory water. It was a gamble that was to abet his financial downfall within two or three years. But he made a determined attempt, with the result that the repertory season instigated in 1950 was to be the second longest thus far in the theatre's history.

Charles Bell formed an association with Winwood Theatres Limited to present a long season of plays. Winwood's name emanated from Hubert Wood and Winifred Payne, both actors who frequently performed in the productions.

They began on 2 January with *Ambrose Applejohn's Adventure*. Among the company, and for several months to come, were Donald Morley, who also directed the first production; Vere Lorrimer, who went on to a long career in television production; Hilary Mason and Peter Bayliss.

Early in the season came *Deep Are The Roots*. Arguably ahead of its time it concerned racial conflict in the southern United States and featured Earl Cameron, the only black actor to see his name above the title in British films of the period.

On 13 February they presented Emlyn Williams' *Night Must Fall*. Playing Mrs Bramson was a revered radio actress of future years, Katherine Parr. A young man joined the company to play the lead opposite her. He had not long finished his national service in Malaya where his participation in troop shows provided inspiration for his services colleague, Peter Nichols, to write *Privates*

On Parade many years later. Beginning with his portrayal of the psychopathic Danny, Kenneth Williams remained a member of the Winwood Company at Devonshire Park for several months.

Meanwhile at the Winter Garden, the Eastbourne public was finding no favour with the Gazette Gossip, referred to as 'Gazza'. When a show was mounted and broadcast on the BBC Light Programme, Gazza's comments almost suggested a return to the censorious style of the previous century. The Floral Hall customers had apparently not entered into the spirit.

'Sunday afternoon's broadcast told the world what we ourselves have known for a long time – that Eastbourne audiences cannot or will not sing. In the first part of the concert, Dick James tried to get the audience to join in with some popular choruses. He is now a sadder and wiser man. A Sunday afternoon Winter Garden audience is as likely to sing "Swannee" as it is to climb up to the top of the Town Hall and hang washing from the flag-post.'

The concert was introduced by Brian Johnston and the star was Eric Barker, whose material was to have ramifications for weeks to come.

Mr Barker made good-natured jokes about Eastbourne's reputation as conservative, reserved and Victorian. They coincided with complaints from 'three young business women' who had come to work in the town and found great difficulty in infiltrating into its social life. Their comments encouraged a volume of support in the correspondence columns, except for the writer of one letter.

'The people of Eastbourne may or may not be snooty (my dictionary is not sufficiently modern to include the word) but they can probably accept the word "Victorian" – for which we in the district should be truly thankful. We don't want to be turned into a second Blackpool, nor – with all due respect to our sister town – do we desire to be as gay as Brighton.'

Hubert Wood and Winifred Payne frequently booked a guest star to appear with the repertory regulars. On 3 April 1950 the bill posters for *The First Year* announced above the title, Anthony Newley, 'the Boy Star of *Vice Versa* and *Oliver Twist*.'

In the first week in May, Jessie Matthews played Eliza in *Pygmalion,* following which another guest artist arrived to star in *Fools Rush In*. Barbara Murray was billed as 'the young Rank starlet'. Kenneth Williams was her husband.

Collectors of show business ironies will note that in Seaside Road, where the Court Players were continuing their season, they were joined at the same time by Hugh Paddick. Was it possible that in the daytime Messrs Williams and Paddick got together on the promenade to develop their Julian and Sandy characters for the future Kenneth Horne radio shows?

Whitsun weekend at the end of May saw the first bank holiday without petrol rationing. This induced an influx of cars to the town and with it the characteristic complaint about day trippers coming to Eastbourne and not spending money. That the first opportunities were being taken by inner-city dwellers to get away from drab worlds to coastal beauties, which the latter's residents could enjoy all the year round, was overlooked. The Eastbourne Gazette echoed the insular attitude in a long editorial but managed – after nearly swallowing its tonsils – to end on a conciliatory note.

'We welcome those who come just because Eastbourne is what it is – even if they come for but a day. We invite them to return – and stay longer.'

Visitors to the theatre performance on Saturday 17 June 1950 were surprised to find who was mingling with them. They were there to see a play entitled *Miss Turner's Husband.* The guest artist was Greta Gynt, who was scheduled to begin a film on the following Monday. Miss Gynt's co-star had just arrived from Los Angeles and had come to see the performance. In the interval a customer at the bar was bemused to find himself rubbing shoulders with the prince of gangster movies. George Raft quietly sipped his whiskey.

Monday 10 July saw the addition of another member to the company, Rosemary Harris, playing in *Ann Veronica.* The same evening, however, found many eyes on the capital. Val Parnell had stalked a particular quarry for a number of years and was now successful. Frank Sinatra began a fortnight's engagement at the London Palladium.

In August Michael Rennie starred in *Goodness, How Sad* at the DPT. Rosemary Harris was already making her mark. Wrote the Gazette:

'For sheer acting ability, Rosemary Harris, as the landlady, Mrs Priskin, is superb.'

Moira Lister arrived in September to take the title role in *Frieda.* In the same month soap came off the ration and at the Royal Hippodrome, taking second billing was 'the funny man from *Ray's a Laugh,*' Peter Sellers. A present-day Eastbourne resident, Hubert Gregg, recalls the crisis in the British film industry in the late Forties. He was lined up for no fewer than four projects and all fell through, which was how he found himself at the Devonshire Park Theatre. He was booked by Hubert Wood and Winifred Payne to do a tour of plays which began at Margate and included Eastbourne. On 24 July 1950 he produced *Life With Father* as well as co-starring with Winifred Shotter. In October he again appeared in *Young Wives' Tale*, but it was the following week's production that stands out in Mr Gregg's memory. He took the title role of *Hamlet* and one of his vivid recollections is of Rosemary Harris as the player queen.

On the afternoon of 9 October, before the first performance, Hubert Gregg was rehearsing alone onstage. The set included a platform to one side, some ten feet above the stage. In his private rehearsal he decided to include a jump from the platform. At the end of his speech following the play scene, he ran up the flight of stairs and jumped off.

Overtaken by dizziness, he lay still in the belief he had crushed every bone in his body. He managed to crawl to his dressing room where he rested for two hours and recovered in time for the first performance.

His exertions were not in vain. Said the Gazette critic of Hubert Gregg's Hamlet:

'He makes every use of the stage to impart action to his work, as in mounting the stairs to the ramparts on several occasions.'

The production of *Hamlet* was the last of the Winwood Theatres season. Charles W Bell then began an association with Harry Reynolds to form the Eastbourne Repertory Company, a leading figure of which was Terence Dudley.

In the middle of that autumn season, the town was shocked by the sudden death of the tenth Duke of Devonshire on 26 November. He was only 55 and on that Sunday morning he had read the Lesson as usual at All Saints' Church, Grange Road. In the afternoon he had suffered a heart attack at home in Compton Place while chopping firewood. His second son, Andrew Cavendish, then aged thirty, took over the title.

The Eastbourne Repertory Company put on their pantomime, *Aladdin*, on 23 December 1950, written and produced by Terence Dudley.

This was a period in which amateur companies could still command large audiences. The EODS could look with satisfaction on its ratings for its two productions at the Devonshire Park Theatre in October and November. A total of ninety members was involved but their customers could not all have been aunts and cousins; their audience numbers totalled 11,400.

For many years Eastbourne's theatres and cinemas had enjoyed significant publicity in the local press. Large advertisements had appeared for each venue. In none of the papers for the first week of 1951 were there any. The Beckett Group put out a statement that the cost of newsprint had increased from £10 a ton pre-war to £41. Printing metal cost had also risen from £23 to £180 per ton. They claimed their advertising rates had increased by 5% but that the local entertainments outlets had asked for a discount. The newspaper group stated:

'In fairness to ordinary traders, we cannot make special concessions in advertising rates to any particular industry.'

Coverage of the theatre scene disappeared altogether including reviews for plays and films. The effect on takings may be judged by the complaint from Jackson Earle at the end of the month's run of his revue *Melody Inn* at the Royal Hippodrome. In April 1951 he declared that the poor audiences were 'due to lack of advertising in the press.' He made a loss of £500.

One townsperson was heard to mutter darkly: 'The town is in the hands of miniature press barons and petty picture house peers.'

Meanwhile a vigorous debate had been taking place in the correspondence columns of the local press questioning the repertory ethos. It was sparked by the signatory 'Disgusted theatre-goer' in the Eastbourne Herald of 25 November 1950, in which he complained of poor houses.

'What kind of shows do the theatre-going public of Eastbourne like? A short while ago Hubert Gregg played in *Hamlet* to an almost empty theatre. It is pitiful to see small audiences for worthwhile plays. Is it possible that Eastbournians are snobs and that only London companies are good for them? If so, then they do not know when they are well off. To them I say:- Come off your high horse and give the repertory companies a chance.'

A second writer echoed the sentiment on 9 December.

'My son is a theatre manager in another part of England and – not being in Eastbourne – his theatre fills. I endeavour to go to the Devonshire Park Theatre every week, and my heart aches for the artists.'

In the same edition another writer resented the 'snob' accusation. 'It seems that because I prefer to watch a First Division football match in preference to say, Eastbourne versus Seaford, I am a snob.'

Clarkson Rose came to the defence of the repertory ideal.

'Repertory companies in Great Britain have never been stronger or better supported than they are today. In Bexhill the Penguin Players have just completed a record season. A little further along at Hastings the Court Players which have been established since before the War play to packed houses.'

Terence Dudley wrote from the Devonshire Park Theatre.

'The Eastbourne Repertory Players have been here for six weeks now. It is true that attendances at the Park Theatre have been poor, but the fact that they are improving is a sure sign that theatre-goers here are not "snobbish" but discerning. Over 300 repertory companies thrive in this country and the number is increasing.'

Mr Dudley was supported by another correspondent.

'If the present company could take up permanent residence at the Devonshire Park Theatre, I feel sure that within the year they would be playing to comparatively full houses.'

The theme of continuity was stressed by Robin A Henderson writing on 23 December 1950.

'A year or so ago an excellent company played for some weeks; after the first week houses were constantly full, and it was a real blow to many of us when the company left.'

The point was backed up by 'Disgusted theatre-goer' who wrote again. 'No doubt the lack of support is due to the fact that no company stays longer than two or three months.'

Raymond Francis wrote from High Bank, Borough Lane.

'It is encouraging to see that Eastbourne's strange apathy towards the professional theatre has caused comment in your columns even if it does not create interest at the box office. Eastbourne is blessed with one of the most delightful of the smaller playhouses in the country. Why it should appeal only to summer visitors is a mystery. Repertory companies have never received from Eastbourne the support they deserve.'

Further spirited defence emerged from the chairman of EODS Dramatic Committee, Mervyn Lambert.

'If the theatre-goers of Eastbourne knew what they were missing by not supporting the present company, the theatre would be full at every performance.'

Nonetheless, the quality of product was about to enter the debate. Said correspondent Percy Gordon in the same edition:

'I fully agree with Mr Clarkson Rose that many famous stars began in repertory. That is the point, they began in repertory, polished themselves up, and became household names much later in their careers. When one wishes to hear a lecture by university professors, one does not go to the secondary school to hear them, although no doubt they received the necessary groundwork there. One looks a little further on for the finished article.'

J William Anstey took the argument a stage further.

'I have always maintained that it is physically impossible to produce a play in a week, especially if the actors are playing in the evenings and rehearsing most of the day. The number of rehearsals is sufficient only to set the movements and a mere outline of the dialogue. The performance which results from the scant preparation is really no more than a memorised reading of the play, aided by the technical resources of the artistes in giving semblance of life to characters which have been insufficiently studied.'

One correspondent had suggested the unthinkable: that forgetting the Eastbourne scene and going to the London theatre was preferable! Mr Francis Hill countered on 6 January 1951.

'A comparison of costs seeing *Black Chiffon* in town and in Eastbourne may be of interest. In town: train fare for two, seats and a meal – £3. To say nothing of time taken – at least from mid-afternoon to midnight.

'In Eastbourne: seats 3 shillings, bus fare 10d, leave home 7pm, indoors 11pm or shortly after. May I also add how much we appreciate the bus which is always waiting outside the theatre after the performance to bring us to the outskirts of Eastbourne.'

Peter Daubeny presented a comedy at the beginning of 1951, after which it seemed the reper-

DEVONSHIRE PARK THEATRE

Lessee and Manager ... CHARLES W. BELL
Secretary ... ERNEST BISHOP Stage Manager ... DICK SELBY
For Charles W. Bell and T. L. Powys Keck

COMMENCING MONDAY, JANUARY 8th, 1951
PETER DAUBENY PRESENTATIONS LTD.
present

THE GAY INVALID

A Comedy with Music and Mime
Adapted from MOLIERE'S " Le Malade Imaginaire "
By Sir BARRY JACKSON and ROBERT BRENON

Characters in the Play :

Valentine, an Officer in the King's Guard	PETER CUSHING
Angelica, elder daughter to Crank	DAPHNE SLATER
Crank	A. E. MATTHEWS
Potion, chemist to Crank	PETER VAUGHAN
Toinette, servant to Crank	ELISABETH BERGNER
Louise, younger daughter to Crank	CAROLINE COMYNS CARR
Belinda, second wife to Crank	HARRIETTE JOHNS
Deeds	ANDREW LAURENCE
Dr. Douche	HUGH PRYSE
Thomas Douche, his son	STUART LATHAM
Heartwell, half-brother to Crank	MICHAEL SHEPLEY
Professor Purge, doctor to Crank	TOD SLAUGHTER

The Italian Touring Players :

Harlequin—WALTER GORE
Scaramouche—GRAHAM STARK. Brigella—PAUL ANSTEE
Colombine—ANNA MACWILLIAM. Chinoise—EILEEN ELTON
Zany—SYLVIA BRIAR

Townspeople ...VICTORIA GRAYSON, CHRISTIE HUMPHREY, LAURIE PHILLIPS

tory system had hit the buffers once more. The theatre closed for three months. An announcement made in the Eastbourne Herald on 28 April suggested that following the debate about the value of repertory, the management could not risk getting its fingers burnt again.

'Monday sees the welcome re-opening of the Devonshire Park Theatre under the management of Charles W Bell. From now on, the policy of the theatre will be to present first-class touring attractions and – as often as can be arranged – plays prior to West End production.'

In a series of stages, advertising and reviews of the shows and films in Eastbourne began to reappear in the local press.

With the re-opening, the spring and early summer of 1951 presented two personal appearances of the old Hollywood variety. A new play, *Storks Don't Talk*, opened on 28 May. Its star was Mischa Auer, a white Russian refugee who had become one of America's most popular film comedians. At a London press reception in the week prior to the opening, he was asked why he had chosen Eastbourne to premiere the play he was to take into the West End. His reply was as follows.

'On a previous holiday trip, I made a fleeting visit to Eastbourne and I have never forgotten the beauty of the town. After the first night of a new play an actor needs time for thought; for that he needs delightful surroundings; for those he needs Eastbourne'.

One can only trust that the writers of the holiday brochure made use of the quotation the following year.

Monday 4 June 1951 saw the opening night of *Dracula*. Taking the title role was Bela Lugosi, twenty-two years after first playing the Count on Broadway. Mr Lugosi stayed for the week with perhaps Eastbourne's only legendary theatrical landlady, Mrs Long of 44 St Leonard's Road.

Bela Lugosi was heading into the last and saddest stage of his career, colourfully illustrated in the 1994 film *Ed Wood*, about the life of the reputedly worst film director of all time.

DEVONSHIRE PARK THEATRE

Lessee and General Manager ... CHARLES W. BELL

JUNE 4th, 1951. For One Week

JOHN C. MATHER and W. H. WILLIAMS
(on behalf of CHARTRES Productions Ltd.)
present

Mr BELA LUGOSI

in a new production of

DRACULA

By Hamilton Deane and J. L. Balderston
Adapted from the novel by BRAM STOKER.

Cast in order of appearance :

Mary Wells (a maid)	JOAN WINMILL
John Harker (Lucy's fiance) ...	RICHARD BUTLER
Dr. Seward (Lucy's father)	DAVID DAWSON
Van Helsing (a famous psychiatrist)	ARTHUR HOSKING
Renfield (a mental patient)	ERIC LINDSAY
Butterworth (an attendant)	JOHN SAUNDERS
Lucy Seward	SHEILA WYNN
Count Dracula	BELA LUGOSI

Decor by Bertram Tyrer

Production and Lighting by Richard Eastham

Edward D Wood Jnr met up with Lugosi not long after the latter returned to Baldwin Hills, California from Eastbourne. As portrayed by Martin Landau in the film, he complained furiously about having to play twelve more performances of *Dracula* in ten American cities. His drug-ridden career ended in a run of Wood's cheapskate movies, finishing with *Plan 9 From Outer Space*.

The following warning appeared in the programme for *Dracula*.

'The Management cannot be responsible for any Patrons who may faint or feel unwell, but First-Aid Attendants are in the Theatre throughout the performance.'

In order to mark the Festival of Britain, three one-act plays by Bernard Shaw were staged in the week of 25 June under the title *Festival Trio*. They featured Terence de Marney and Winifred Shotter. During the same week a shoe-string tour of a new play by Christopher Fry entitled *A Sleep of Prisoners* arrived for presentation on three nights in St Saviour's Church. Four young actors appeared in it. Two of them have never been heard of since; the other two were Stanley Baker and Denholm Elliott.

20 August and week at the Park played host to a curiosity entitled *Ladies Night in a Turkish Bath*. Focussing on one member of the cast, the Eastbourne Herald declared:

'Hughie Green is the young shy professor who gets trapped in a turkish bath on the wrong night.'

The following week had local audiences bracing themselves. For the first time they were able to see Tennessee Williams' *A Streetcar Named Desire*. Vanda Godsell was Blanche Dubois, Paul Carpenter was Stanley, and appearing further down the cast list was Michael Bryant.

October saw another General Election and the return of Winston Churchill to power. Locally, Winifred Shotter's brother-in-law, Charles Taylor, was returned with a twenty thousand majority over Christopher Attlee, the Prime Minister's son.

Raymond Francis was travelling daily to London from his Borough Lane home to report to the newly-opened Lime Grove television studios. He played Dr Watson in a six-part Sherlock Holmes serial. His local audience on successive Saturday evenings would not have been sufficient to fill the Devonshire Park Theatre itself. At approximately the same time it was calculated that in the Eastbourne district the number of television license holders totalled 740. If the theatre had known poor houses at various times, the cause had certainly not been competition from the nine-inch screens.

The 1951 Christmas pantomime was presented by Stanley Willis-Croft. Among the pre-publicity items for Dick Whittington the Eastbourne Herald observed:

'Billy Howard as Sarah the Cook and Benny Hill as Idle Jack will be responsible for the two main comedy roles: both are well-known broadcasting artistes.'

The paper also announced that the return rail fare to London would be increased to 19/2d (96p) in the new year.

The Eastbourne Herald of 5 January 1952 included a short biography of Benny Hill.

'He is heard on the West Regional programme every Monday evening in a series of concerts given at Forces' camps. The Monday evening broadcasts are recordings, the actual performance taking place on the Sunday, and Benny Hill, who is under contract to the BBC, has to spend much of that day travelling from Eastbourne to places like Plymouth and Yeovil. A little strangely, eight of his broadcasts have been heard on the Third Programme.'

On 12 January 1952 after the last pantomime performance, the Devonshire Park Theatre again closed and did not open until Easter Monday. The reason did not become clear until October and it was to herald the most far-reaching change in the theatre's history since its 1884 opening.

For the moment, business recommenced on 14 April with *Nuts In May* starring Lupino Lane. That Easter week was a family affair in Eastbourne, for at the Royal Hippodrome a production of *Me And My Girl* was presented, starring Mr Lane's son, Lauri Lupino Lane. It had been Lupino himself who had created the role of Bill Snibson in the original Victoria Palace production.

Following Christopher Fry's *Ring Round The Moon* starring Helen Haye and Alan McClelland, Stanley Willis-Croft presented the first long summer variety season at the Park for many years. *Summertime Serenade* starred Avril Angers and featured a nineteen year-old Jean Bayless. It opened on 16 June and ran until 20 September.

In the following week, *Smilin' Through* played for a week and marked a return visit by Hazel Court and Dermot Walsh. Then, for the second time in 1952, the Devonshire Park Theatre went dark and stayed so until Christmas, except for a couple of EODS productions.

The Royal Hippodrome held the fort, first with a September production of the *Carroll Levis Teenager Show*. It was compered by a young artist known then by her real name of Violet Pretty. Within a short time she would change it to Anne Heywood.

A further development occurred at the Royal Hippodrome which would have ramifications for the Devonshire Park Theatre. To the Hippodrome Frank Barnes and his wife Elizabeth Gilbert brought their English Ring Actors from Penzance, which had been their base. They began a ten-week season beginning 27 October.

In the week they opened with *The Barretts of Wimpole Street*, Gracie Fields made an eagerly anticipated appearance at the Winter Garden, immediately prior to her participation in the 1952 Royal Variety Performance.

On 1 November the Eastbourne Herald gave notice that the Council were offering their tenants the opportunity to buy their own homes, some thirty years before Margaret Thatcher adopted the idea nationally. Any tenant taking part in the scheme would be required to pay a deposit of £100 and instalments of £47 a year for twenty-five years.

Also that November, the Ambassadors Theatre was the venue for the opening of a routine thriller by Agatha Christie, starring Richard Attenborough and Sheila Sim. It was called *The Mousetrap.*

What then was happening to the Devonshire Park Theatre in a year that had seen it closed for months at the start and end of 1952 as well as the first part of the year before?

The lessee of the theatre was still Eastbourne Theatre Limited. It will be recalled that the lease had been taken out in 1936 for a period of twenty years. Immediately after the War they had awarded the sub-lease to Charles W Bell, which was scheduled to expire in July 1953. Mr Bell could not make it that far. In 1952 he went bankrupt, hence the long months of darkness at the theatre.

At the same time the Duke of Devonshire was saddled with £6 million death duties following his father's demise in 1950. Already plans were in hand to sell the Eastbourne estate, Compton Place. The Duke was the major shareholder in the company still owning the DPT: the Devonshire Park and Baths Company, by now called Devonshire Park Eastbourne Limited.

Eastbourne Corporation saw their chance. The Herald of 6 December 1952 reported that negotiations to take over the lease – begun in July – had been completed in October. Eastbourne Corporation became the lessee, taking over from Eastbourne Theatre Limited, at 11 o'clock on the morning of Friday 5 December 1952 when the keys changed hands. The Town Clerk released the official statement.

'The Eastbourne Corporation have become occupiers of the theatre until 9 May 1957 and will provide and secure provision of, in this theatre, entertainment for the enjoyment of residents and visitors in keeping with the high reputation of the town as a resort.'

At the same time the Town Council instructed Mr F H Busby, the Town Clerk, to begin negotiations immediately for the acquisition of the freehold. This was not the first time of trying. A bid had been made in 1946. In order to pay for the freehold, the Corporation's Capital Account would have had to be used. In order for that to happen, permission needed to be obtained from the Ministry of Housing and Local Government. The Ministry had refused to give its permission in 1946.

George Hill, who was already manager of the Winter Garden for the Corporation, now became the general manager of the Devonshire Park Theatre. Under his, and the Corporation's, auspices the theatre reopened for the pantomime on Christmas Eve 1952. *Cinderella* was presented, featuring Fred Wynne and Pamela Cundell.

The final stage of the ownership story would take another few years but eventually the moment came. Eastbourne Corporation finally acquired the freehold of the Devonshire Park Theatre on 25 March 1957.

VIII

Repertory Settles In

Eastbourne Corporation embarked on their first year as the sole lessee of the Devonshire Park Theatre. In spite of the debate that had taken place on the repertory ethos, and notwithstanding indifferent box office response, the policy was decided. The evidence was that repertory companies were the norm across the nation in 1953 and Eastbourne was to be no exception. Thus it was that the Devonshire Park Theatre began a period of almost continuous repertory work that was to last for the better part of a quarter of a century.

The first company to begin a protracted period was the English Ring Actors. As we saw in the last chapter, they had already undertaken a ten-week season at the Royal Hippodrome. The Corporation now took them on and transferred them to the Park.

The director of English Ring Actors, Frank Barnes, explained his thinking.

'The intention is to found a permanent repertory theatre during the Eastbourne winter season. We want to cater for the residents of the town. That is why prices have been reduced and monthly tickets made available. The essence of enjoyment of repertory comes from seeing each week's production.'

Frank Middlemass

The first play was *Temple Folly* on 20 January followed by *Berkeley Square*. The latter was directed by a regular member of the company, twenty-four year-old Michael Blakemore who was, according to Barry Bourne of the Eastbourne Herald: 'in the third year of his visit to England from his homeland, Australia.'

The monthly tickets referred to by Frank Barnes for price reductions were announced in the programme for the 3 February production, *Captain Carvallo*.

'Season Tickets Available for Four Weeks
Commencing February 17th.
4/6 seats 15/-; 4/- seats 13/6; 3/6 seats 12/-

One of the company members was Frank Middlemass. Not only did he act but he was the stage director for several productions. Mr Middlemass had begun his career with English Ring Actors at Penzance in 1949. Nearly fifty years later his memories of the period are still clear and especially so of his time at the Devonshire Park Theatre. Fellow actors he recalls vividly include John Arnatt and Mysie Monte.

As referred to earlier, Mr Arnatt was from Friston, and engagements at the Park enabled him to continue to see his parents. Miss Monte went on to achieve the distinction of being the longest-running player in *The Mousetrap*. She it was who portrayed the luckless Mrs Boyle – the first to take the long drop, at the end of Act 1 – for ten years in the Fifties and Sixties.

The first season was one of five months. Programme acknowledgments show how much reliance was placed on local businesses for props and stage settings. On 17 March, for instance, *The Seventh Veil* was presented and the programme stated:

'Furs kindly loaned by David Jackson, Grove Road.
Miss Gilbert's Hand-woven Skirt by "Harlequin", Cornfield Road
Furniture by the Grand Hotel.

Who would even dare to use furs today, let alone acknowledge where they came from?

Following a two-month break, the English Ring Actors returned in August 1953 with *Johnnie Belinda*. One of its cast of twenty was Frank Pettit. Their run lasted through to the following May. Joining them at the time was Alun Owen who went on to write television plays of distinction, of which perhaps *No Trams To Lime Street* is particularly recalled.

Local man Raymond Francis appeared in several productions including *On Approval*. Margaret Diamond starred in N C Hunter's superb Chekovian piece, *Waters of the Moon* in the week beginning 19 January 1954. Miss Diamond was to emerge as one of Dirk Bogarde's blackmailers, Miss Benham, in the breakthrough film of 1961, *Victim*.

The April production of *The Magic Cupboard* featured Vi Stevens (Terry Scott's 'mother' in *Hugh And I*) and Jack Howarth, later of *Coronation Street* fame.

The English Ring Actors' last production of the season was *Anastasia,* featuring Helen Haye, Leonard Sachs, Alun Owen and the first television 'William Tell', Conrad Phillips.

In the 5 January 1954 programme, a complete list of the theatre staff was included. Among them was 'Evelyn Harmer – Usherette, Upper Circle'. Evelyn figures later in the story and she was still at the theatre until just before her death forty years later.

During the periods when the English Ring Actors were taking a break, the touring productions continued. In the week of the Queen's Coronation, Clarkson Rose brought back his *Twinkle* company, featuring Billy Burden. Later that June, Linnit and Dunfee presented *As Long As They're Happy with* Jack Buchanan and Dorothy Dickson. In July Hermione Baddeley appeared in *Murder Mistake*n, directed by Judith Furse, and in the following week *Whodunnit?* starred Claude Hulbert and Enid Trevor. Playing the small part of Signor Ferrari was Robert Stephens.

The spring and summer of 1954 presented some fascinating projects and names. There was a production of *The Archers*, still only three years old on the radio. The future 'Ethel' from *EastEnders*, Gretchen Franklin, played Mrs Perkins.

Two favourites still of the Devonshire Park Theatre, Michael Denison and Dulcie Gray, appeared with Richard Goolden in the 'prior to London' production of *We Must Kill Toni*. The following week, the same management, Ralph Birch, put in *The Soldier and The Lady*. It starred the American actor, George Colouris. Mr Colouris had featured in Orson Welles' classic, *Citizen Kane,* ten years earlier but had settled in this country in the early Fifties. *The Soldier and The Lady* also starred Peter Cushing, this in the same year that he was to make national impact as Winston Smith in the first television showing of *1984*. In the cast too was Sheila Sim, whose brother Gerald would feature in two years' time in the story of the Devonshire Park Theatre.

Those Fifties years involving both touring and repertory productions provide many names of people who were then bit-part actors but who in time progressed to significance in their profession. One example occurred during the week of 26 July 1954. A comedy entitled *A Horse, A Horse!* was presented by Hugh Wakefield: the same Master Hugh who had so convinced as a schoolboy half a century earlier.

Reference to the programme extract shows that a small part -with the unlikely name of 'Tops, of the BBC' – was played by David Baron, who was also assistant stage manager for the touring production.

David Baron had been in repertory and on tours for about eight years. He was within ten years of becoming a playwright of international acclaim. Before forsaking the boards and taking up the pen, he reverted to the name he had been born with in Hackney: Harold Pinter.

Mr Pinter has confirmed that in the week of the production he received his first inspiration of significance to his playwriting success. He was staying in digs in Ashford Road. A motley assortment made up the household led by an eccentric landlady. One of the other guests described himself as an 'out-of-work concert pianist'. These people were to provide the seeds for Pinter's first major play, *The Birthday Party*.

The English Ring Actors returned for the late summer and autumn of 1954 and the top price ticket returned to 5/6d ($27^1/_2$p). For that money audi-

DEVONSHIRE PARK THEATRE
EASTBOURNE

General Manager .. .. .. GEORGE HILL

Week commencing Monday, July 26th

HUGH WAKEFIELD PRODUCTIONS LTD.

presents

A Horse! A Horse!

A Stable Fable by L. du GARDE PEACH
(Author of "The White Sheep of the Family")

The following have arrived:

Morgan, *the Butler*	W. P. LIPSCOMB
Maggie Bennett, *Visitor*	ANNE RICHMOND
Duchess of Wistburgh	DORIS HARE
Lady Sarah, *her Daughter*	GILLIAN LUTYENS
Hon. Ronnie Lochvitie	TOBY PERKINS
Duke of Wistburgh	HUGH WAKEFIELD
Sam Pringle, *Circus Proprietor*	CYRIL SMITH
Jo, *of the B.B.C.*	SHIRLEY WATSON
Tops, *of the B.B.C.*	DAVID BARON

Persimmon by Hilarity out of Thespio
Trainer .. .. Charles L. Fox, Holborn

Visitors to the Abbey:
Daphne Rogers, Sydney Palmer, Betty Trueman, Arthur Ranscomb, Muriel Latham, Claude Hughes

The Play directed by FRANK SHELLEY

The action of the play takes place in a room at Wistburgh Abbey, the family seat of The Duke of Wistburgh. Time: The Present.

ACT I A Winter Morning

ACT II The same day. Evening

ACT III Some days later. Afternoon

Design by VIC
Scenery by MAYFAIR DISPLAYS LTD.
Decor by VIOLET SEYMOUR
Theme Song, "A Horse! A Horse!" by FRANK SHELLEY

Nylon Stockings by Keyser Bondor. B.B.C. equipment and effects by Bishops Sound. Mr. Wakefield's pipe, lighter and tobacco by Dunhill's. Hunting boots by Tuezek. Miss Hare's evening gown and dresses by Harvey Nichol. Miss Lutyen's evening gown and dresses by Maud Connell. Gin by Booth's Distilleries Ltd. Virginia Cigarettes by Abdulla.

Stage Director	Geoffrey Salisbury
Stage Manager	Anne Richmond
Assistant Stage Manager	David Baron

(For Hugh Wakefield Productions Ltd.)

Business Manager	Geoffrey Salisbury

July 1954

ences were introduced to further unknowns such as Jean Marsh, long before she teamed up with Eileen Atkins to create *Upstairs, Downstairs*. In the week beginning 16 November a young actress was hired to play in The Little Hut. It was only a year later that the same actress, Sylvia Syms, signed a seven-year contract with Associated British and starred in her first film, *My Teenage Daughter*, with Anna Neagle.

The rep company led by Frank Barnes and Elizabeth Gilbert soldiered on through to April 1955. A diversity of productions was offered from Kenneth Horne's light comedy, *A Lady Mislaid*, to Goldsmith's *She Stoops To Conquer*. All through this period, even though the Devonshire Park Theatre's own orchestra had long gone, live piano music was an essential ingredient of the evening out. It was provided by an Eastbourne favourite going back to the war years, Dorothy Atlee.

Advertisements in the programme could also lend themselves to the artistic touch. Consider, for instance, the enticing offer of food following a performance.

'When the final curtain falls
And you leave your box – or stalls,
'Ere the evening is done
Drop in at the Sally Lunn for suppers 50 Meads Street'

Truckloads of film and theatre stars continued to draw up on Mondays at Compton Street during the non-repertory weeks. Moira Shearer played Sally

Bowles in *I Am A Camera*. Jessie Matthews appeared in *Private Lives*. Coincidentally, a week later, her one-time sister-in-law, Binnie Hale, arrived to play in – not inappropriately – *It's Never Too Late*. Perhaps Katie Boyle was the first television name to go a-touring, in *Pardon My Claws*.

At about that period, the ten year-old Clive Francis became besotted with theatre. He took to spending his Saturday afternoons crouched at the stage door shyly asking for autographs. On 9 May 1955, A E Matthews opened for a week's run in *The Manor of Northstead*. The following Saturday afternoon Clive was in position. The great 'Matty' emerged after a performance. By then he had become extremely old and short-sighted. Upon seeing young Clive proffer his dog-eared programme, A E Matthews threw his arms around the boy and said: 'Ah, Gladys, thank God you came round.'

One of the English Ring Actors' plays featured Reginald Tate who had appeared in 1951 as the first television Bernard Quatermass, ahead of its time and causing a national sensation. In the same play, *A Call on the Widow*, was a young actor, John Stone, who was lined up to appear the following year in *Quatermass II*. Not long after his week at the Devonshire Park Theatre, Reginald Tate died suddenly and the sci-fi professor in the 1956 sequel was taken by another DPT regular, John Robinson.

The English Ring Actors appear to have made their final appearance at the Park on Saturday 27 August 1955 with a play entitled *The Red-Headed Blonde* featuring Roderick Lovell.

On Christmas Eve 1955, another great repertory name, Arthur Brough, arrived to take over proceedings for three months. He began with pantomime. For *Treasure Island* he hired an up-and-coming stage and television actor to portray Long John Silver. Subsequently, Robert Eddison rose in prestige at the Old Vic and National Theatres.

Throughout the winter and spring of 1956, Arthur Brough presented productions for Crest Plays and his director was Michael Gover. The reputation of Arthur Brough in those days can be gauged by the pre-publicity of a production of *Bird In Hand* in the week beginning 27 February. The leaflets declared grandly: 'Mr Brough will play the lead'.

A study of programme selections during the repertory seasons provides hints of the rapport that existed between the company and community it served. At the end of Arthur Brough's season the following note appeared in the programme of his last offering, *High Temperature*, week beginning 2 April 1956.

'Mr Brough and Mr Gover wish to take the opportunity of thanking all those who have so kindly loaned properties and furniture during their season at the Theatre, and to wish them, and all our patrons a Very Happy Easter.'

Another round of touring productions set in including Tom Arnold's presentation of *Mr Kettle and Mrs Moon*. The young director he chose went on to a very different kettle of fish a couple of months later. He was Tony

Richardson and the play he directed at the Royal Court Theatre was *Look Back in Anger.*

1 October 1956 saw the return of Michael Gover, who had been Arthur Brough's assistant. He had now formed the Michael Gover Players and they were to be in residence for the next two years. The first production under the new auspices was *Carrington VC*. One of the small parts was played by Clive Exton. An ASM of the time was Jill Hyem. Both were to become distinguished writers of radio and television drama.

During the summer months the programme price had increased 100% from threepence to sixpence. Mr Gover brought it back again to threepence on 22 October. A close watch was kept on prices generally. For the pantomime, *Jack and the Beanstalk*, the top ticket went up to 7/6d but was back to 5/6d when once the company plunged into the new year season of 1957. Concessions were offered at the rate of two for one on Mondays, half price for senior citizens at both matinees, and a season ticket deal. At a top price of 18/- (90p) one could see four shows.

In January 1957, a young actor called James Lloyd joined the Michael Gover Players for six weeks. Among the plays he did were *I Lived With You* by Ivor Novello. The Eastbourne Herald of 30 January said the following about him.

'James Lloyd in Novello's own part as the prince sailed through this terrific role like an old stager. His approach to the part, his understanding of the complex character he has to portray marks Mr Lloyd as an actor of quality. Monday night's audience loved the play. The twelve-strong company had to take three curtain calls and even then young James Lloyd had to wait quite a while for the applause to subside before he could thank the house for their appreciation.'

James Lloyd decided not to pursue an acting career. He dabbled in television, co-presenting *Wish You Were Here* with Judith Chalmers for a while. But his interest in folk music set the seal on his future. Folk on Friday in 1970 was the forerunner to Folk on Two which, under the name of Jim Lloyd, he produced and presented on Radio 2 for more than twenty-five years.

It was on *Folk On Friday* that Jim Lloyd met the original producer, Frances Line. In time she was to become Controller, Radio 2. Upon her retirement the couple moved to Eastbourne and became members of the Friends of the Devonshire Park Theatre. In 1997 Frances and Jim Lloyd celebrated their Silver Wedding anniversary.

A special note in the programme for week beginning 8 July 1957 declared: 'During the Summer the Plays will change on THURSDAYS.' Holiday trade in Eastbourne at the time was still booming and Michael Gover spotted that by such a changeover day, the week-long stayers might be inspired to see two plays. The procedure is still applied in the Nineties when, even with a reduced holiday trade, the theatre reports especially healthy business on summer Thursdays.

That 8 July 1957 production was *Separate Tables* starring Raymond Francis. His son, Clive, who was by then at the newly-opened Ratton School, had graduated from crouching outside the stage door, autograph hunting, to being allowed to sit in on some of the dress rehearsals. These occasions provided much interest and stimulation as they were the first professional rehearsals he had seen at close quarters. Because Michael Gover used to get irate, his language was not as sweet to a twelve year-old boy's ears as his parents would wish. So, recalls Clive, such trips were curtailed!

One actor who was in at the start of Michael Gover's residence was Gerald Sim. He also co-directed the first production, *Carrington VC* in October 1956. The following month he directed on his own *Murder on the Nile*. He spent a total of eighteen months at the Devonshire Park Theatre.

Gerald Sim has since become a familiar face in films and television but at that time he was consolidating his position as a young repertory actor. From Mr Sim we have a clear picture of what life was like working in weekly rep.

He has kept an old school note book filled with every production in which he has been involved, and he reports that there are forty-seven listed for Eastbourne in the late Fifties. Looking back now he supposes that weekly rep was a unique experience.

'You discarded a play as soon as the Saturday night performance was over. Not consciously of course, but it just drifted away as you concentrated on the next one. Inevitably there were a few parts that I loved and would happily have played for far longer than a week. I liked particularly a play called *The Shadow of Doubt*, and also *Plaintiff in a Pretty Hat* by Hugh and Margaret Williams. He, being an actor himself, wrote some lovely dialogue that was a joy to do.'

Mr Sim recalls people too, in particular James Beck, who would go on to national fame as wide boy Private Walker in *Dad's Army*.

'He was a remarkable actor – only young at the time but he had an extraordinary ability to play characters who were much older than himself, believably. I remember him so well in South Sea Bubble in which he gave a lovely performance. I always felt he would go far. Such a tragedy that he should die so early.'

It will be seen from the programme illustrated here that James Beck played Gerald Sim's father! Notice also local Eastbourne man, Stephen Brewer's involvement, and to what extent repertory companies relied on local traders.

Gerald Sim found Michael Gover enthusiastic and encouraging.

'But he kept us up to scratch. It was particularly important to him that we looked all right. In those days every actor and actress in a rep company had to use their own clothes, their own wardrobe, and use them every week. How the girls managed to ring the changes I don't know, but even the men had to have quite a few suits and jackets and trousers, and above all an evening dress. That would seem so odd today because I don't think many young actors in tele-

DEVONSHIRE PARK THEATRE
EASTBOURNE

General Manager .. .. .. GEORGE HILL

Week commencing Monday, April 29th

Monday—Friday at 8 p.m. Saturday 6 and 8.30 p.m.
Matinee: Wednesday at 2.30

MICHAEL GOVER *presents*

SOUTH SEA BUBBLE

By NOEL COWARD

Cast in order of their appearance:

John Blair Kennedy (*Boffin*) .. MICHAEL GOVER
Captain Christopher Mortlock (*A.D.C.*) STEPHEN BREWER
Sir George Shotter (*Governor of the Samolan Isle*) RAYMOND SOMERVILLE
Lady Alexandra Shotter (*his wife*) MARY KEAN
Punalo Alani (*father of Hali Alani*) JAMES BECK
Sanyamo (*a Butler*) .. .. HAYDN WARD
Edward Honey (*the Colonial Secretary*) CHARLES HERDMAN
Cuckoo Honey (*his wife*) .. BRIDGET CLAIRE
Admiral Turling .. .. TREVOR BAXTER
Mrs. Turling (*his wife*) .. MARGARET ROY
Robert Frome (*the Chief of Police*) JOHN KERR
Hali Alani .. .. .. GERALD SIM

Play directed by DOROTHY CLEMENT
Set designed by NEVILLE USHER
Entr'acte Music by Dorothy Atlee

The action of the play passes on the island of Samolo, a British possession in the Pacific Ocean.
The time is the present.

ACT I		**The verandah of Government House**
ACT II	**Scene 1**	**The same (a few hours later)**
	Scene 2	**Hali Alani's beach house (a few hours later)**
ACT III	**Scene 1**	**The verandah (the next morning)**
	Scene 2	**The same (a few hours later)**

The undermentioned kindly loaned by

FURNITURE
Messrs. Dickeson & French, Ltd., Memorial Square.
Messrs. Bobby & Co., Ltd., Terminus Road.
Messrs. Green Bros., Hailsham
Messrs. Stephen Bindon Ltd., Pevensey Road.

PROPERTIES
Messrs. Austins Ltd., Cornfield Road.
Messrs. Bobby & Co., Ltd., Terminus Road.
Messrs. Goddard, Cornfield Terrace.
Mrs. Hopwood (at Mathers), Cornfield Road.
The Grand Hotel, Grand Parade.
Messrs. Tyler, Grove Road.
Messrs. Cains, Cornfield Terrace.
Messrs. June Broadhurst, South Street.
Messrs. Lowins, Junction Road
Messrs. Moorcrofts, South Street.
Messrs. Jensons, Cornfield Terrace.

ELECTRICAL FITTINGS
Messrs. H. Beney & Sons, South Street.

JEWELLERY
Messrs. Shipton & Co. Ltd., Terminus Road.

RECORDS
Messrs. Boyds, Seaside Road.

FLOWERS
Messrs. Scotts of Eastbourne (Flowers) Gildredge Road.
Lighter by Ronson
Nylon Stockings by Kayser.
Olivier Cigarettes by Benson and Hedges

April 1957

vision possess anything but a pair of jeans and a sweater. They are clothed for everything. I remember Michael was particularly keen that all the men in the cast had clean shoes – if it was that sort of play and often it was. It was the sort of detail that mattered to him. And he was a stickler about the girls shaving under their arms! Quite right of course – it was important that we looked as good as possible.'

By the time he arrived at the Devonshire Park Theatre, Gerald Sim had been working in fortnightly and weekly repertory companies for eleven years, since leaving the Old Vic in 1945. Some of the forty-seven plays he went on to do at Eastbourne were familiar to him. In a hard-working season that was a bonus. The study was so much easier and an actor had more confidence about them.

'Most actors like working at the seaside. Eastbourne is an attractive pleasant place and on summer afternoons many of the cast would go down to the beach to learn their lines. But I found there were too many distractions and it didn't really work for me. I was asked to judge the beauty contest on one occasion but that was different.

'I met a lot of people in the street who were very sweet and encouraging and came regularly every week on the same night. I was often asked the question about whether I preferred Comedy or Drama. I could only answer that I really didn't have a preference – that it was the one I was doing at the time. In that sense rep was fun because there was a constant mix of plays.

'One elderly couple did actually say to me, rather apologetically, that they hadn't really enjoyed the previous week's play very much so they were going to give it a miss this week! Which was rather sad because they were obviously going to miss the very play they would have liked since it was a complete contrast to the week before.'

A part of Gerald Sim's weekly routine was to drive on Sunday morning to Hove where his parents lived. He had to be back early on Monday morning but he recalls the complete break it afforded.

Gerald Sim

His Eastbourne digs were comfortable with a large bedroom where he could pace around learning his lines. His landlady introduced him to scrambled egg with cheese on top. He had never come across it until then, but thereafter became an addict. He had his share of congealed meals under a tin lid on the stove but admits that was his fault.

'I don't suppose my experiences at Eastbourne differ substantially from many other actors at that time. It will never happen again. Many actors today will never know what they missed so it won't matter to them. But the variety of work we did and the experience of working with audiences, has been a tremendous help to me in films and television. Anyway it is nice for me to think back on. The Devonshire Park Theatre had a pleasant atmosphere, was about the right size, comfortable, and had rather good acoustics. A very happy and contented time of my life.'

The late spring of 1957 provided a break for the Michael Gover Players and further touring productions came the Park's way. One week Eastbourne audiences could revel in the glorious sight of Margaret Rutherford as Lady Bracknell in *The Importance of Being Earnest*. In another week they received *Look Back in Anger*. This was the original English Stage Company's production presented less than a year earlier at the Royal Court Theatre, Sloane Square, directed by Tony Richardson and starring Alan Dobie and Michael Bryant. One can but wonder if the general manager of Eastbourne theatres, George Hill, experienced sleepless nights preceding the play's run.

Selected productions provide a hint of the tugs of social interest of the Fifties, as is the case in any age. John Osborne was writing about his concerns and speaking for the new brand of Angry Young Men of England. Yet less than a year later, Michael Gover presented *Act of War*, described as 'a new play by Peter R Newman about a company of British soldiers cut off in jungle during the initial Japanese invasion of Burma'. John Osborne might well have been preoccupied with anger, but this was only thirteen years after the end of the Second World War, and for many men back from the Far East, wounds – and memories – were still fresh.

Michael Gover's company returned for a final burst of six months' repertory in June 1958. It was a play-safe season to round things off, with productions of *Busman's Honeymoon*, *Random Harvest*, *Love From a Stranger* and *Dear Delinquent* providing the diet. Mr Gover brought in several guest artists. Barry Sinclair and Elsie Randolph appeared in *Silver Wedding* and Fay Compton played Mrs St Maugham in *The Chalk Garden.*

A young actor arrived on 15 September 1958 to play small parts and be an assistant stage manager for the last season. His name was Rodney Bewes and he was the only company member to overlap, albeit briefly, the next stage of the Devonshire Park Theatre's history.

IX

The Couple from Bexhill

In the latter half of 1958, Richard Burnett and his wife Peggy Paige were invited by the Corporation to stage a Christmas pantomime and follow it with a three-month repertory season. They stayed for eleven years.

They had established the Penguin Players at the De La Warr Pavilion, Bexhill in 1950 and by the late Fifties were presenting the same productions at the Assembly Rooms, Tunbridge Wells. Both had been actors for many years, and we have seen that Peggy Paige had been a member of the Royal Hippodrome Players as far back as 1935.

It was therefore on Christmas Eve, 1958 that *Aladdin and His Wonderful Lamp* opened for a season of no more than a week and a day. It was devised, written and supervised by Richard Burnett. It will be noted from the cast list that Rodney Bewes stayed on to play one of the Chinese policemen.

Immediately after the last performance on 3 January 1959 the theatre closed for the rest of the month for redecoration. But as the programme showed, a season was promised shortly and it began on Monday 2 February with Oscar Wilde's *Lady Windermere's Fan*. Among the early productions, *I Killed The Count* featured Ron Pember, who went on to appear in the television *Secret Army* and to become a director for Vanessa Ford Productions.

DEVONSHIRE PARK THEATRE
EASTBOURNE

General Manager	George Hill

Wednesday, 24th December at 8 p.m.
Friday, 26th December until Saturday, 3rd January
2.30 TWICE DAILY 8.00

Aladdin & his Wonderful Lamp

Written, Devised and Supervised by Richard Burnett

Characters:

Immortals:	
Fairy Goodwill	Edwina Day
The Slave of the Lamp	Hubert Rees
Mortals:	
Aladdin	Patricia Kilgarriff
Widow Twankey	Frank Woodfield
The Emperor of China	Kenneth Burnett
Princess Baldroubadour	Julie Michaels
Abanazar (*a Wicked Magician*) ..	Vernon Joyner
The Grand Vizier	John Citroen
Wishee-Washee (*a Laundry Boy*) ..	Derek Smith
Prince Pekoe	Eve Brown
So-Shi	Linda Bennett
Ah-Tish (*a bad Chinese Policeman*) ..	Douglas Harris
Ah-Tosh (*a worse one*)	Rodney Bewes
First Soldier } and Charley	Colin Greene
Second Soldier } (*the Horse*)	David Henderson-Tate

Chinese Boys and Girls, Spirits of the Cave, Harem Girls, etc.:
Anne Asher, June Barnett, Jennifer Beresford, Shirley Gover, June Hall, Lee Knight, Janet Lee, Shirley Poole, Pamela Sutton, Sandra Wood, Janet Wynveldt, Jennifer Wynveldt
The above are pupils of The Eastbourne School of Dancing

The Pantomime produced by Frank Woodfield
Original Lyrics and Music by Richard Burnett, Mary Hargreaves and Douglas Addey

A young actress who was to feature in several plays was Julia Foster. A few years later she would star with Tommy Steele in *Half a Sixpence*. Sometimes the Burnetts brought in guest stars but essentially the Penguin

Players concentrated, as did most repertory companies, on a regular band of actors.

Live piano music continued to be a nightly feature and for years Dorothy Atlee had provided the service. Miss Atlee returned to the al fresco productions of Cecil Johnson's Fun In The Air at the Redoubt Gardens, and the entr'acte music was taken over by Mary Hargreaves and Douglas Addy. The following appeared in the August 1959 programme.

'Special notice: Miss Hargreaves and Mr Addy
will be pleased to play request numbers.
(All requests to be handed in at the box office.)

On Boxing Day 1959, Richard Burnett presented his second pantomime which saw a return to the Park of one of the great dames of the genre. Clarkson Rose was no longer presenting *Twinkle* but he was still entertaining audiences the length and breadth of the country. Dorothy Atlee returned to direct the orchestra.

By March 1960 another full season of weekly rep was in full swing. During that month the Penguin Players presented Robert Munro's *The French Mistress*. By that time David Hemmings had made a reputation as a jobbing boy actor. The Children's Film Foundation had made ample use of his services, and he had also featured in the 1958 film version of *No Trees In The Street*. Now he was at the Park playing Edmunds, the head boy. Within six years David Hemmings would achieve international fame as the star of Antonioni's Sixties cult film, *Blow Up*.

A social breakthrough occurred in the summer of 1960 while the Penguin Players were taking one of their well-earned breaks. During the July week when Hugh Sinclair and Mary Kerridge appeared in Graham Greene's *The Complaisant Lover*, the note in the programme 'Smoking Permitted' appeared for the last time. Sarah Churchill's arrival to play Eliza in *Pygmalion* on Monday 18 July coincided with a notice in the programme in thicker print: 'Patrons are requested not to smoke during the action of the play.'

The slightly renamed Penguin Productions Ltd were back in August. Richard Burnett took on as stage director and small part player a big man. Robert Bridges would go on to a long and esteemed run as the Beadle in the original production of *Oliver*. Richard Murdoch and his daughter Jane guested in *The Reluctant Debutante* in September.

A touring production arrived to play the week that Richard Burnett was busy preparing his third pantomime. It was the week that *Coronation Street* began on Granada Television. The period was now very much one of the television age. Its influence had rocketed in the ten years since the estimate that only 740 licenses were held in Eastbourne. A decade later Max Bygraves was watched by twenty million viewers nationwide in *Sunday Night at the London Palladium*. Unlike the situation in 1950, television, with the addition of the commercial channel, was now a competitive force to be reckoned with.

Was it therefore a ploy by Eastbourne Corporation to bring in a touring production with special competitive value? The supporting cast of *The Geese Are Getting Fat* read like a theatrical 'Who's Who'. Avice Landon, Michael Trubshawe, Peter Barkworth, Eynon Evans, Joyce Heron, Simon Oates and Bobby Howes were all on the payroll. A curious link connected the star and the play's director.

Michael Wilding had known what it was to be a Hollywood Name. Only four years earlier, he and his then wife, Elizabeth Taylor, had given a dinner party while the filming of *Raintree County* was in progress. One of the guests, Montgomery Clift, had left early. An hour later, in the pitch dark of a deserted Californian hillside, Michael Wilding had tried, along with his wife and Rock and Phyllis Hudson, to free Clift from an horrendous car crash which would cause him permanent disfigurement.

Now, Michael Wilding, divorced and back in Britain, was on the touring circuit being directed by Nigel Patrick, one of Taylor's and Clift's co-stars of *Raintree County*.

Christmas 1960 saw not one but 'Two Grand Comedy Pantomimes'. Penguin opened *Sinbad The Sailor* on Boxing Day, and *Mother Goose* on 2 January. Pantomime is notorious for evincing hectic times. Frequently the King sits upon a throne sticky with fresh paint at dress rehearsal, or even on the first night. To get a second pantomime organised a week after the first must have caused frenzy.

In the second, Julia Foster was Fairy Godmother. Joining the company for a short season was Mark Langridge, now one half of Langridge and Sayers: not a comedy act but a men's outfitters in Old Town. Mark featured in *Come Away Death*, presented on 20 February. That production provided the first of several guest appearances for Penguin Productions by Derek Bond. Mark Langridge comes from a theatre family. His sister, Avril Francis, still gives strong performances today in non-pro companies in Eastbourne.

In between Penguin seasons, the tours continued to roll. They included *One For The Pot* on 17 July 1961, billed as 'Immediately prior to presentation at the Whitehall Theatre.' An array of the best-loved names in farce came to

Compton Street, having established themselves not only on stage going back almost to the end of the Second World War, but throughout the monthly live televised comedies on Sunday nights in the 'Laughter at the Whitehall' series. Here they all were, together for one week at the Park: Brian Rix, Leo Franklyn, Basil Lord, Terry Scott, Sheila and Peter Mercier, Larry Noble, Helen Jessop and Hazel Douglas.

In one of Brian Rix's volumes of autobiography, *Tour de Farce*, he outlines the special difficulty he had with the play during the week's run at Eastbourne. In *One For The Pot*, he played four identical brothers. With the clever use of doubles, the audience could be persuaded into believing Mr Rix was on one side of the stage, although after he had gone off, he would seem to reappear from another part of it altogether. The movement involved required the future Lord Rix to be fleet of foot to an unsurpassed degree – even for him. He needed constantly to dash behind the set ready for his next entrance. At Eastbourne the situation was far worse, as he explains in his book.

'You see, the stage at the Devonshire Park is very shallow, so the set was hard up against the back wall, which meant that instead of running round the stage, as I changed from one brother to the next, I had to gallop out of the nearest exit into the dressing-room corridor, race along the corridor – cutting a swath through any unfortunate passers-by, come tearing in at the furthest entrance to the stage, screech up to my point of entry and rejoin the frolics convulsing a happily confused audience. It was very exhausting, at all times in fact, but particularly so at Eastbourne.'

Two weeks later another Whitehall company arrived. *Simple Spymen* was billed as 'Direct from $3^1/_2$ years at the Whitehall Theatre'. John Slater starred and Andrew Sachs featured. Among the other cast was a young actor making his way: Timothy West. The company manager was Bertram Parham who had been an actor himself. He had appeared at the Devonshire Park Theatre as far back as November 1936 in *Love From a Stranger*. The day it opened at Eastbourne, 2 November 1936, coincided with the first television transmission from Alexandra Palace when Elizabeth Cowell introduced Adele Dixon singing a special song for the occasion. One has the impression of the cast gathered in a DPT dressing room that night and declaring: 'It'll never catch on.'

Many years later Timothy West recalled how useful and knowledgable a man Bertie Parham was. Visitors' books in theatrical digs were notorious for coded messages to pass on to the following week's players. For instance, if a compliment of any sort was entered but was followed by the words 'quoth the raven', an explicit warning was being given not to touch the place with a barge pole.

Timothy West had begun to notice on various tours the initials L.D.O. appearing in visitors' books. They occurred frequently and he was baffled, so he asked Bertie Parham what the letters meant. 'Landlady's daughter obliges,' came the reply.

The Whitehall companies having returned to Trafalgar Square or continued their touring, Richard Burnett and Peggy Paige continued their own now well-established repertory work. The couple were becoming a part of the community and in January 1962 they addressed the first of many letters to their patrons in the programme as follows.

'Ladies and gentlemen: we are glad to have the opportunity to thank you for the very warm reception which you have given to the members of our new company. They are all extremely happy at the prospect of playing a long season in this delightful theatre and hope to provide you with many evenings of most enjoyable theatre-going.'

Thereafter a paragraph or two always appeared providing notes about the following week's production. This appears to indicate the first time that theatre programmes at the Park expanded beyond a cast list and synopsis of scenes. Given that they still cost no more than 6d (2½p), one may argue, as the writer will later, that possibly this represented the beginning of a slippery slope to the extravagant and pricey brochures of today.

Another change occurred during the spring of 1962. Up to then, all Penguin productions opened on Tuesdays. They were now to do a full week and the last Tuesday opening was on 17 April. The play was *The Young in Heart* which featured Isobel Metliss, still a regular at the Devonshire Park with her work for Newpalm Productions.

In the 4 June programme for *Black Coffee* is an apparent first reference to a theatre club. By the 1960s, such clubs for regular theatre-goers were springing up across the country. In the course of the Burnetts' weekly letter, the idea was slipped in.

'By the way, if you have not yet joined the Eastbourne Theatre Circle and would like to do so, or would like to know more about it, will you please write to Miss Joyce Marks, Hon Secretary, c/o Winter Garden.'

The policy of including special guest stars in repertory weeks continued. 20 August saw the production of *Distinguished Gathering*. The title befitted its star. Vic Oliver, originally from Vienna and maintaining his accent to the end, was a big name. Once the husband of Sarah Churchill, he had starred at the Palladium and worked regularly with the equally renowned Ben Lyon and Bebe Daniels. He seems to have favoured Eastbourne considerably. From the 1930s onwards Vic Oliver's name crops up in programmes at the Royal Hippodrome, Pier Theatre and Winter Garden. While he was playing in *Distinguished Gathering*, building was in progress a short distance away to construct the Congress Theatre. When it opened the following year, Mr Oliver was one of the first stars to appear there.

For some unspecified reason the company appeared under various guises in the programme. They were known as Penguin Players, Penguin Productions or – as from August 1962 – Eastbourne Repertory Players.

Under whatever name, Richard Burnett and Peggy Paige presented every production in 1962. No weeks were taken up with touring companies, and such policy was set for the following years with a few exceptions.

A Penguin favourite, Richard Murdoch, arrived to play the Dame for the Christmas season. The programme for *Puss in Boots* is of interest in that it sees a further addition to content. Mention has been made of the personal messages from the proprietors, by then firmly established. Now, apparently for the first time, biographical notes were included of some of the cast.

RICHARD MURDOCH as Queen Isabella

Born at Keston, Kent, Richard Murdoch made his first stage appearance in "The Blue Train" in 1927. He played in Cochran's revue "Ballyhoo" and other West End musicals in the 1930s and was in the cast of "Band Waggon" at the outbreak of the war. From 1939 to 1945 he served in the R.A.F., during which time he broadcast in the popular radio show "Much Binding-in-the-Marsh". Has since appeared in many British films and the recent radio series "The Men from the Ministry".

JUDY CORNWELL as Princess Pearl

This talented young TV and stage actress commenced her training with dancing lessons at the age of three, shortly afterwards going to Australia with her parents, returning to England when she was twelve. Has appeared in the name part of "Cinderella" in Brighton, Aberdeen and Croydon. TV shows include "Dixon of Dock Green" and Radio shows "The Navy Lark". Her ambition is to become a writer. She has already written several short stories and is at present working on a TV play.

Programme notes, Christmas 1962

In the same programme an advertisement appears inviting customers to buy from Caffyns a Morris Mini-Minor for £435.11s.3d including purchase tax.

There was no hanging about in those days. The pantomime finished on Saturday 5 January 1963 and the next rep play, *Guilty Party*, was onstage three nights later. Its programme offers another first. Personnel of Eastbourne Corporation began to be credited. The General Manager, George Hill, had always been named, but so too from now on were his deputy, Ernest J Fulcher and the House Manager, Jimmy Fox.

The new stage director in January 1963 was Geoffrey Stanfield who was to work for many years at the theatre. He continues to design productions for Eastbourne Operatic and Dramatic Society.

A sobering note was included in a January programme from Richard and Peggy Burnett, hinting at the 1962/63 winter conditions, the worst since 1947.

'May we thank you for the many messages of congratulation we have received about our pantomime, *Puss in Boots*. Unfortunately the terrible weather played havoc with our audiences, but we are glad to know that none the less the show gave much enjoyment.'

Week beginning 26 March 1963 saw another new arrival at the Devonshire Park Theatre. Still a resident of Eastbourne today, Jo Sands continues to be noted for her non-pro company work. Then, as Joanna Sands, she became an assistant stage manager and was promoted to stage manager only two months later. She was to remain in that capacity for several years. In an interview for the Eastbourne Herald at the time, Joanna declared she had no ambition to become a great actress. She would prefer to make her name as a good stage manager or director ('rather an unusual field for a woman', observed interviewer Barry St John Neville) but considered marriage and a family more important. Joanna achieved all her ambitions and became a great actress too.

Writing in the Eastbourne Herald more than thirty years later, Jo Sands paid tribute to the set designer for both Michael Gover in the Fifties and throughout Richard Burnett's tenure.

Neville Usher was regarded as a superb scenic designer and artist. No mean feat, declared Miss Sands, when weekly rep necessitated tearing down one set on Saturday night and having a new one up and ready to open for Monday evening. Actors and stage managers all liked and admired Neville Usher whose wit – together with patience – on fit-ups was legendary. He was known to repaint an entire set on a Monday because a visiting actor 'couldn't act on a set painted green'. His scene dock was the old Devonshire Park racquets courts and his work was of the highest artistic standard. Jo Sands believes that Eastbourne repertory audiences were privileged to have had for the many years he worked at the DPT a resident designer of outstanding talent. Neville Usher always commuted from his home in Brighton and it was there he died in 1996 at the age of 86.

3 June 1963 saw the opening performance of *The Two Mrs Carrolls*, for which Eric Lander was brought in as a guest star. A popular actor of the time, Eric Lander had become a national figure as Lockhart's assistant, Baxter, in television's *No Hiding Place*. They were the Morse and Lewis of their day. The Morse equivalent was played by Raymond Francis whose son, Clive, was now beginning his own career. Having progressed from autograph hunting at the stage door, being allowed to sit in on dress rehearsals in Michael Gover's days, and appearing with EODS, Clive Francis had been taken on as an assistant stage manager by Richard Burnett and Peggy Paige. Eric Lander's visit to the theatre to play Geoffrey Carroll in Martin Vale's drama is embedded in Clive's memory. He takes up the story.

'I was put on grams. In those days all sound effects were on record and usually there was quite an assortment, making it always hard to drop the needle on the exact spot and at the right time. *The Two Mrs Carrolls* is set in the south of France. At the end of the play Geoffrey Carroll has a row with his wife and tells her he is going to leave. "Nothing you can do can stop me," he says. "I shall jump into my Aston Martin, race to Monte Carlo and play the tables." With great elan, he leaves the stage, slamming the door. Meanwhile I sit nervously with my needle poised over the right track to lend atmosphere to the moment with a screech of tyres on the gravel and the mighty roar of the powerful Aston Martin as it races down the drive.

'One night after Eric had made his heroic exit: "I shall jump into my Aston Martin ...." etc, the baleful sound of a horse and cart could be clearly heard clipclopping down the gravel path. Collapse of audience and of play.'

As a young man, Clive Francis also suffered from an acute stammer, so whenever he went on the book -as prompter – he put 'the fear of God' into the rest of the company. Only God must have known what it did to Clive.

He rates himself as a truly hopeless ASM, forgetting constantly to set vital props which he would then brazenly hand to members of the cast, in the hope that they would secretly place them in the appropriate place. During one Agatha Christie thriller, he forgot one evening to set the murder weapon which the Inspector would reveal in front of the entire cast.

'About a page before this nail-biting moment arrived, and after I had seen the prop gun still sitting, glaring at me, on the offstage table, I crawled on my hands and knees up to the french windows (mercifully there are always french windows in an Agatha Christie). I tugged at the trouser leg of the nearest actor who, rather alarmed, bent down and pretended to tie up his shoe lace. He took the offending prop and passed it behind his back to another actor who did likewise until it was placed within the Inspector's reach just at the appropriate moment of revealment.'

Richard and Peggy Burnett were always thrilled to welcome back one of their own who had gone on to make good. This was clearly evidenced in the programme letter preceding week beginning 1 July 1963.

'Ladies and gentlemen: Our play next week is one of the most outstanding successes of the London stage for many years, the famous *Billy Liar* by Keith Waterhouse and Willis Hall. We are extremely pleased to welcome in the main role one of the leading young actors of the English stage: Derek Fowlds. Derek actually started his career with us in this theatre a few years ago, appearing in such plays as *Alibi* and *As Long As They're Happy*. Since then he has made a name for himself in films and on the London stage particularly in the plays *The Miracle Worker* and *How Are You, Johnny?* Immediately after playing with us in Billy Liar, he is leaving for New York, where

DEVONSHIRE PARK THEATRE
EASTBOURNE

General Manager - - - George Hill
Deputy General Manager - - Ernest Fulcher

Telephone: Eastbourne 121
Box Office open weekdays 10 a.m. to 1 p.m. and 2.15 to 9 p.m.

Commencing Monday, 1st July and during the week

Monday to Friday at 8 p.m. Saturday at 6 and 8.30 p.m.

Matinee Wednesday at 2.30 p.m.

EASTBOURNE REPERTORY PLAYERS'

present

BILLY LIAR

By KEITH WATERHOUSE and WILLIS HALL

Characters in order of their appearance

Florence Boothroyd	**Molly Veness**
Geoffrey Fisher	**Paddy Ward**
Alice Fisher	**Mary Gauntlett**
Billy Fisher	**Derek Fowlds**
Arthur Crabtree	**Derrick Slater**
Barbara	**Tani Bentis**
Rita	**Amy Mitchell**
Liz	**Helen Cope**

Produced by ROBERT NORMAN

he is to take one of the leading parts on Broadway in *Chips With Everything* by Arnold Wesker.'

Rep life continued apace with the Eastbourne Repertory Players as the 1960s moved on. The fare on offer was usually light comedy or thrillers but sometimes they were of deeper substance. David Chant twice played Percy in *Rattle of A Simple Man*. Charles Dyer's play portrays an innocent north country lad, in London for the Cup Final and he allows himself to be taken home by Cyrenne, a prostitute. David Chant recalls civil war breaking out in the foyer when the play was presented.

Mr Chant joined the company in September 1963 and stayed for its remaining five years. He had come from Her Majesty's Theatre, Barrow-in-Furness where he had designed and painted all the sets as well as acting in the productions. He settled into life in Eastbourne where he still lives.

One statistic he holds firmly in his mind is the five audience members who died in mid-performance during his five years at the Devonshire Park Theatre. In one case, someone succumbed in the very front row. The curtain was brought down, the deceased carried out and the play resumed. For some reason, Mr Chant recalls the play in question as being *The Gioconda Smile*.

He also remembers patrons who were very much alive. In the middle of a thriller, there was a blackout followed by a gunshot. In the silence he distinctly heard someone announce in the dress circle: 'I'm just going to the loo.'

David Chant was noted for his character work and he played young and old regularly. His first appearance, for instance, was as Derek Bond's father in *The Tulip Tree*. He recounts another occasion of audience participation. While playing one of the leads in *The Odd Couple*, someone near the front of the stalls commended him with the observation: 'Isn't he good for his age?'

He is not the only actor to have observed how efficient the acoustics are from the auditorium to the stage. The message clearly is: Don't risk saying anything during a performance – you will be heard!

One of the actresses who stands out in David Chant's memory is Mary Gauntlett. She was a powerful, sensitive performer whom he played opposite when they took the leads in Ted Willis' *Woman in a Dressing Gown*. The production was the subject of discussion for an evening organised by the Eastbourne Theatre Circle. Two hundred members were in the theatre on 8 February 1965 when the two actors and director joined them to debate the issues raised in the play which had not long been performed.

After five or six years of repertory slog, David Chant found that with recent marriage and a new mortgage, the time had come for more stable employment. He became an art teacher, specialising in ceramics, at Cavendish School, Eastbourne, from where he retired in 1995.

By the early Sixties, another theatre man had come to reside in the town. Ronald Shiner was a much loved comedy actor, popular in all branches of the entertainment world. Richard Burnett persuaded him to make the short journey from his home in Meads to play Alfred P Doolittle in *Pygmalion*. The audience in the packed house on opening night on 2 November 1964 included Sandy and Kay Powell, and Clarkson Rose.

Ronald Shiner was responsible for one of the most illustrative examples of the dangers of long-run-itis. Brian Rix spoke of it from the stage of the DPT itself on the Sunday he and his wife, Elspet Gray, provided an evening of entertainment to commemorate the tenth anniversary of the Friends of the Devonshire Park Theatre in 1994. *Reluctant Heroes* had been going for more than two years at the Whitehall Theatre with the same squad playing it night after night. One evening somebody dried. Four of them were onstage including Mr Shiner. The prompt came in but there was no response. Believing the actor concerned had not heard, the prompt delivered the line again though louder. Still no response evoked a further and even louder delivery. Ronald Shiner turned to the corner in exasperation.

'We know what the line is, but 'oo says it?'

Mention of Clarkson Rose is a reminder that near the end of his long life he made two more appearances at the theatre, one of which was the centenarian, Henry Mellowes in *The Full Treatment*, in February 1966.

ALADDIN

Characters in order of their appearance:

Abanazar	GEOFFREY LEA
Slave of the Lamp	DAVID CHANT
Fairy Goodwill	ELIZABETH POWER
Ah Tish	RICHARD BURKE
Ah Tosh	RICK CRISP
Grand Vizier	NEWTON JONES
Prince Pekoe	CAROLE CARTER
So Shi	VIVIEN HULBERT
Wishee Washee	KEITH VARNIER
Widow Twankey	**OLIVER FISHER**
Charley	BEVERLEY WALLER, BARBARA CHILTERN
Aladdin	**CHRISTINE EDMONDS**
Princess Baldroubadour	LEONIE SCOTT
The Emperor or China	ANTHONY BAIRD
Ping Pong	MARY GAUNTLETT
Attendants and Bearers	DAVID MUSTARD, TERRY BARHAM, JANET SAYNER, SUSAN WOOD
Principal Dancer	BEVERLEY WALLER
Corps de Ballet	JUDITH BANKS, JOE BRIDGER, MARY HOLLOWAY, ANN LEDGER, AVRIL LANGRIDGE, SONIA PERRY, SUSAN WOOD, BARBARA CHILTERN, JANET SAYNER

(The dancers trained at the Sussex School of Dancing)

PROGRAMME OF MUSIC

ACT I

NEW YEAR'S DAY IN CHINA	Hargreaves and Addey
LOVE MAKES THE WORLD GO SQUARE	Rodgers
HERE COMES ALADDIN	Hargreaves and Addey
THAT'S WHAT I'D LIKE FOR CHRISTMAS	Ornadel
SIDE BY SIDE	Ager
MILLIONAIRE-O	Hargreaves and Addey
OUR MIGHTY EMPEROR COMES	Hargreaves and Addey
THE EMPEROR OF THIS LAND	Hargreaves and Addey
Reprise: MILLIONAIRE-O	Hargreaves and Addey
A SPOONFUL OF SUGAR	Sherman
ROYAL LAUNDRY MAIDS	Hargreaves and Addey
I HEAR MUSIC	Berlin
BALLET (from "Kismet")	Borodin
THE CAVE IS OPEN WIDE	Hargreaves and Addey

From two old stagers, let us turn to a youngster of the time just starting out. Elizabeth Power was seventeen years old and she had just won a place at the Royal Academy of Dramatic Art. In the holidays she came back home to her parents at Eastbourne. During one such break she knocked on the stage door of the Devonshire Park Theatre to ask if there was anything she could do. Within a short while she was, variously, assistant stage manager, tea girl and wardrobe assistant. On one occasion she remembers operating the lighting box whilst the electrician went on stage to play a small part.

'But that's what it was like in those days,' recalls Miss Power. 'Weekly rep and everyone had to turn a hand.'

Her first appearance was as

Fairy Moonbeam in *Jack and the Beanstalk*, Christmas 1964. Among the cast were regular company members Vilma Holingbery as Jack and Michael Napier-Brown as Simple Sammy. The husband and wife team were eventually to go to Northampton where they have established a long successful career.

The following year's pantomime, *Aladdin*, stands out in Elizabeth Power's memory. As Fairy Goodwill, she had to sing 'A Spoonful of Sugar' before a front cloth while a scene change was going on. Something went badly wrong though she cannot recall what it was. It meant she had to do the entire song again. She feels certain the children must have found it irksome by the time she had finished!

Elizabeth Power

Elizabeth Power summed up her feelings about her student days.

'Those holiday jobs at the Devonshire Park were bliss to me. I was in a real theatre with professional actors – and they all treated me as an equal. I was delighted to come back and do *Murder Once Done* and *Brief Encounter* in the mid-Nineties. The Devonshire Park Theatre is a joy to play in – there is an atmosphere and a smell about those old theatres. Years of greasepaint and thunderflashes leave memories behind.'

20 June 1966 marked the end of an era. From the moment the theatre had opened eighty-two years earlier, the telephone number had comprised three digits: 121. The box office was now to be called up on Eastbourne 21121.

In parallel there was a fourth change of name, with the players now called the Devonshire Park Theatre Company. The supporters' club, the Eastbourne Theatre Circle, evolved into the Devonshire Park Theatre Club with Vic Ellis its president and Jerry Christian as chairman. A note in one programme announced that David Galer, Curator of the Towner Art Gallery, would address the Club on 13 February 1967 on the subject: 'Artists in the Theatre World'. New members would be welcome.

A heartfelt plea on the theatre's behalf appeared in the Eastbourne Herald when its editor, Eric Redfern, wrote the following in January 1967.

'Now is the time of year when the Devonshire Park Theatre Company faces the winter struggle for survival – the time of the year when weekday audiences slump to mini proportions and the vast bulk of Eastbourne theatre-goers stay at home hugging the fireside and devouring television.

'The time of the year, indeed, when Devonshire Park and the gallant company which keeps the stage flag flying, deserves every bit of box office support it can get. And doesn't get it!

'Making allowances for cold dark evenings and all the hazards of an English winter, it is difficult to explain just why Eastbourne, with its proud reputation as a town which pays generous tribute to the arts, should be so meagre in appreciating the Devonshire Park Theatre Company when November comes.

'There is of course a good solid core of supporters who go along to the theatre every week to watch and applaud their favourites. But it is very much a minority group. There are many many evenings when the players perform to yawning rows of empty seats.

'Few serious students of the theatre would challenge the statement that Richard Burnett's resident company gives excellent value for money. Through the winter months the plays chosen for presentation are many and varied. A goodly mixture of highbrow and lowbrow, in fact, within reason something for everyone.

'The theatre fans who stay away ought to realise that more towns than not of Eastbourne's size are without their own resident theatre. Up and down the country there are dozens of cities and towns which have nothing regular to offer in the way of stage entertainment.

'But despite the apathy and apparent disinterest, Mr Burnett's company tackles the task in hand with commendable enthusiasm. Among them there is the sort of cheerful, practical approach which ought to convince many more people that regular visits to Devonshire Park can become a most happy habit.'

Had we not seen such articles before – ever since 1884 in fact?

It has been noted that among all the thrillers and frothy comedies there would be an occasional excursion into something more challenging. It had happened with *Rattle of A Simple Man*. It happened again on 9 October 1967. In the preceding programme letter, Richard Burnett apparently felt the need to warn his audience diplomatically.

'On Monday 9 October *The Killing of Sister George* will open at this theatre – the recent London comedy success from the Duke of York's and St Martin's Theatres. The play was awarded the Evening Standard 1966 award as the best play of the year and has played with enormous success not only in England but in America and indeed all over the world. It is an amusing and adult story centred around June Buckridge, an actress who has made an enormous reputation playing the part of "Sister George" – a district nurse in a popular radio serial. The sudden decision to terminate the serial and kill off the character of "Sister George" coincides with the break-up of June Buckridge's own private life, and there is much pathos as well as comedy in the telling of this very frank and modern story.'

An innovation of Christmas 1967 was the presentation for the first time of Richard Burnett's pantomime at the four year-old Congress Theatre. He brought back Richard Murdoch to star in *Dick Whittington*. A touring company took over the Park for the week commencing Boxing Day.

Richard Burnett and Peggy Paige began 1968 with another change of name and a new policy. On Thursday 1 February the production company under the title Theatre South-East opened for business with a new musical, *Found in a Handbag*. It was a musical version of *The Importance of Being Earnest*. As ever Mary Hargreaves and Douglas Addy were on hand to take care of the musical direction. In the programme, Richard Burnett introduced Theatre South-East. As will be seen from the reproduction here, it was designed to present each play in both Eastbourne and Bexhill. A show would open at the DPT on Thursday, close on the following Wednesday and open again the next night at the De La Warr Pavilion.

Productions in 1968 included *Richard of Bordeaux*, *Dear Brutus*, Wait Until Dark and Ustinov's *Photo Finish*. Otherwise the diet was Agatha Christie thrillers and Jack Popplewell comedies.

The policy continued into 1969, which was to prove the last year of residence for Richard and Peggy Burnett. A firm link with later years was forged in a brief programme note in January, which ran as follows.

'Among those appearing next week in *A Song at Twilight* will be Daphne Palmer, a delightful and well-known actress who has now joined our company.'

Daphne was to become one half of Newpalm Productions which would still be presenting summer seasons at the Park thirty years later.

The programme for *The Circle* presented on 15 May 1969 was the last of the small 7 inch by 5 variety, which had been in existence since the late Forties. The following week, patrons read about *Blithe Spirit* in the new 9 x $5^1/_2$ inch format. This too was to become familiar to audiences and would remain for nearly thirty years. The traditional eight pages increased to twelve, the price doubled from 6d to one shilling and biographies of company personnel were featured on a regular basis.

This may have been arguably the moment when the rot set in. Theatre programmes

THEATRE SOUTH-EAST

This new play-producing organisation has been formed by an amalgamation of the Devonshire Park Theatre Company of Eastbourne and the Penguin Players of Bexhill. Its productions will be seen in Eastbourne and Bexhill, and later in other selected towns in the South-East of England.

The new arrangement will enable one large Company to offer at each theatre a weekly change of programme by a regular interchange of plays. Actors, Actresses, producers, scenic and stage-management staff will have a minimum of two weeks rehearsal instead of one week.

The choice of plays will be widened, and this big step forward in theatrical service to the two towns will mean more exciting and satisfying evenings at their theatres.

The directors of Theatre South-East appeal strongly to all playgoers in this part of the country to give regular support to their productions, and to encourage others to do the same, so that the company can long continue to offer them the delight and inspiration that only the living theatre can bring.

continue to grow in size, density and price. Gone are the days when they provided no more than a cast list, synopsis of scenes and a note of the following production. They can no longer be obtained at low cost and stored in a small shelf space. If the fare on offer is no more than a Christie thriller, the programme buyer is likely to be treated to half a dozen pages of discourse on murder through the ages, whether he/she wants it or not. Where once a programme cost three to four per cent of a top ticket price, it is now often eleven per cent.

Saturday 30 August 1969 saw the last performance of *Let Sleeping Wives Lie* by Harold Brooke and Kay Bannerman. It was the final performance of Theatre South-East and of Richard Burnett and Peggy Paige's long tenure at the Devonshire Park Theatre. The letter in the programme, reproduced here, explained all.

A LETTER FROM THEATRE SOUTH-EAST

Ladies and Gentlemen,

Our regular supporters will know—and visitors to the town will perhaps be interested to learn—that this is the last production in this theatre by this management—at any rate for some time.

We have now been in continuous occupation of the Devonshire Park Theatre for over ten and a half years, as well as presenting two Summer seasons of plays at the Royal Hippodrome and occasional productions at the Congress Theatre. During this time we have presented more than five hundred different productions in Eastbourne, including eleven pantomimes and some half-dozen musical plays. The range of authors represented has, of course, been extensive and includes Ibsen, Shaw, Thornton Wilder, Arthur Miller, Tennessee Williams, Pirandello, Jean Anouilh and many others of a similar calibre among the more 'popular' writers—indeed any playwright whose works we thought would appeal to a good proportion of playgoers in the town.

During the coming Autumn and Winter our companies will be operating in Bognor Regis and in Bexhill, and next year in Folkestone as well, and we hope that any of you who find yourselves in these towns will care to come in and renew acquaintance with our shows.

Meanwhile we extend our warmest thanks to each and all of you for your support during our long stay in Eastbourne—and also and particularly to all the talented artistes and members of the staff who have worked so hard to achieve such excellent results.

Yours sincerely,

RICHARD BURNETT
PEGGY PAIGE

Several significant goodbyes took place that night. As explained earlier, Neville Usher had designed and built the sets for many years. He took his leave along with Mary Hargreaves and Douglas Addy who had always been on hand to provide the entr'acte music before the play and during the intervals.

The end may have come suddenly. The new beginning came just as quickly.

X

The Man in the Green Velvet Jacket

Monday 1 September 1969 saw the presentation of the first local repertory production by Mr Charles Vance. He was to stay at the Devonshire Park Theatre for six years.

Charles Vance had already had a colourful career. He had been an actor for twenty-three years and a producer for another nine. An Irishman by birth, he had known what it was to be a contract player in Hollywood. At one stage Paramount had paid him twenty-five dollars a week to appear in westerns and utter lines such as: 'Saddle 'em up and we'll cut 'em off at the pass.'

He returned to Britain at the end of the Fifties and during a week playing in *Rebecca* at Hythe, he met his future wife, Imogen Moynihan. Eventually they came to Eastbourne to form the Eastbourne Repertory Company.

The inaugural production was *Watch It, Sailor!* This was the sequel to *Sailor, Beware!* by Philip King and Falkland Cary. Kay Woodman played Emma Hornett. Following on closely, she played in *The Lodger*, together with her husband, Valentine Dyall, who was for years associated with the play.

Included in the first programme was an invitation to join the Eastbourne Theatre Supporters' Club. Not long afterwards came an appeal for heavy fabric furnishings!

CAN YOU HELP US ?

In weekly repertory we have great difficulty in obtaining a stock of CARPETS, RUGS, CURTAINS and CUSHIONS. People often tell us that if they had only known, they could have let us have some which they were discarding. Although past their best for use in the home, they can still be effective on stage.

If you have any CARPETS, RUGS, CURTAINS or CUSHIONS you do not want and would like to help us, if you will let us know, we will send someone to collect them. Thank you.

THE EASTBOURNE THEATRE SUPPORTERS' CLUB

MEMBERSHIP OF THE CLUB GIVES **YOU** MANY ADVANTAGES AS A THEATREGOER—MEMBERSHIP OF THE CLUB GUARANTEES A STRONG FUTURE FOR THE EASTBOURNE THEATRE COMPANY—WHY NOT JOIN TODAY?

To: CHARLES VANCE,
DEVONSHIRE PARK THEATRE,
EASTBOURNE

Please enrol me as a member of the EASTBOURNE THEATRE COMPANY SUPPORTERS' CLUB. I enclose my first annual subscription of 10/-.

In one of the early programmes too there appeared an advertisement that must have tested the patience of the audiences. The building of South Cliff Tower had caused a storm of protest. Now it was being emphasised how successful the selling of its flats had been.

It was in the first full year of residence, 1970, that the Eastbourne Repertory Company made its mark. Classics ancient and – at the time – modern were presented in the weekly repertory programme. On Monday 9 March *The Merchant of Venice* was presented with an increased cast clearly exceeding the usual number of company players. They included one, Eric Richard, brought in to play Balthazar and Stephano. Many years later Mr Richard would achieve national recognition as Sgt Bob Cryer in *The Bill.*

Elsewhere the year featured productions of Robert Bolt's *Flowering Cherry*, Moliere's *The Impostor*, and Waterhouse and Hall's *Billy Liar*. *Hedda Gabler*, *Dracula*, *The Prisoner* and *Johnny Belinda* were also selected. The latter was directed by Charles Vance who played Belinda's father, emphasising that he was a 'hands-on' actor/manager.

In April there was a presentation of *Stop The World, I Want to Get Off*, the cult musical by Anthony Newley and Leslie Bricusse. The two leads were played by Jimmy and Gilda Perry. By then Jimmy Perry had come to be known nationally as the co-writer of *Dad's Army*, and at the time of his appearance as 'Littlechap' in the musical, further series were being prepared. Jimmy and his wife Gilda had much in common with Charles and Imogen Vance. They had spent nine years from 1956 running the Palace Theatre, Watford before Jimmy found national success through his script-writing.

In the Eighties Jimmy Perry would present a series of television shows from the Devonshire Park Theatre itself, featuring individual entertainers including Spike Milligan and Jimmy Edwards.

Christmas 1970 presented two seasonal shows for the price of one. *Aladdin* opened on 24 December featuring as Widow Twankey Charles Simon, who was still being billed as the last Dr Dale from the long-running radio series. *Aladdin* was preceded by *Beauty and the Beast* for one week. Included in the cast was a young Roger Tolliday who, years later, would bring his own company, Corpus Productions, to Compton Street.

Also taking up residence at the same time as Charles Vance was a pianist who would come to hold a secure place in the hearts of DPT patrons. As earlier stated, the piano had always been taken seriously and a full programme prepared for every show. The production programme itself would list the pieces of music to be played before the curtain went up and in the two intermissions (as there always were in those days). This was continued when Harry W Tait joined the theatre but the music was extended to include the Devonshire Park Theme. It was written by Mr Tait himself based on a suggestion by Allen Christie, the lifelong professional partner of Jack Tripp. Long after Harry Tait's retirement, the Devonshire Park Theme was played on tape following the National Anthem to accompany the audience's departure from the theatre.

Harry W Tait

1971 saw the innovation of what was to become an annual event: the Summer Festival of Theatre. Three plays were presented in rotation, changing on Monday and Thursday, allowing week-only holiday-makers to see two productions. One of the company, Dennis Spencer, has since noted that if someone was very eager, he could see all three by dashing in on the Saturday of his arrival in Eastbourne.

Although there would be many changes in personnel, the entire six years saw Charles Vance's company presenting every production and no complete week ever saw the Devonshire Park Theatre dark, even in the struggle-for-custom days of January and February. The two months, from 28 July to 18 September, must therefore have come as welcome relief to the company. The constant drudgery of learning lines every week came to a stop for seven weeks in the summer, allowing actors some breathing space.

In an interview with the writer in 1996, Dennis Spencer spoke of the requirements of the ideal repertory player.

'You needed actors who could learn lines. It was no good being brilliant. If you were the most brilliant actor in the world but couldn't learn your lines quickly, you were useless. But a producer would try to balance the load. If he'd given an actor a big part one week, he'd try and give him a smaller one the week after.

'It was also an advantage if, like me, you had played weekly rep in many theatres. In my case I'd often played for Charles – still do, all these years later – and if he suggested a play I'd done before, that made it an easier week.'

Mr Spencer went on to speak of the 'autumn trough'. The three rotating plays for the summer festival played to packed houses most nights. When the visitors left at the end of the season and before the big numbers returned for the pantomime, there was a dip in custom, echoing the situation of many earlier years.

Unsurprisingly, therefore, it was decided that presentations in November and December 1971 would begin on Wednesday evenings. The selection provided a marked contrast to the summer season fare. The one-man offering, *Brief Lives*, featured a repertory regular, Anthony Linford. Peter Shaffer's *Five Finger Exercise* and Arthur Miller's *The Price* were in the programme together with *The Hollow Crown.* An occasional added problem was that plays were also presented sometimes at the Congress Theatre. As *The Glass Menagerie* opened on Wednesday 24 November 1971, *Conduct Unbecoming* was already in full swing next door at the big venue, starring Mark Wynter and Eric Lander.

The early Seventies moved on and weekly rep continued. Dennis Spencer relishes the days.

'People got to know you in different guises. They would come into the theatre wondering who you were going to play this week. They would tell you which of your performances they liked better than others. It was like local football. You had support for the team. And Charles usually got himself a good team because he's a very clever man for casting; and that meant there were followers of the team.

'It could be so supportive that I remember what happened at Hastings when I worked for Harry Hanson's Court Players. We used to take the curtain and across the footlights would come fifty cigarettes, perhaps for me, or a bottle of whiskey for the character man, a bunch of flowers or a box of chocolates for the leading lady. People had their favourites and enjoyed giving them gifts. I always thought this showed a wonderful spirit.'

Joining 'the football team' in 1972 was Amanda Wilkins who had just finished two years at Nottingham Playhouse. She joined the staff as Charles Vance's production assistant. Amanda recalls the time as a fun-filled period.

'I typed the contracts, did the copy for the programmes, proof-read them and paid the artists. My mother and I had a flat in Pearl Court close by and had as lodgers Dennis Spencer and Wendy Brierley. We used to have first-night parties when all the company would come back for a meal, and I do remember several of us would go down late at night if it was hot for a plunge in the sea.'

It would seem that the first-night parties provided the only respite. Dennis Spencer recalls the pattern of weekly rep life at Eastbourne, as in any town.

'10 o'clock Tuesday morning, you arrive to read next week's play, having done the first performance the previous night of the current play. The director's sitting out front and he tells us where we're going to move and what the set is going to look like. He tells his stage management what he wants obtained for the production. Poor Eastbourne is then bombarded by young girls or boys asking to borrow settees and everything else from shops to make the sets look good.

'We'd finish plotting the play 1.30 to two o'clock. On Wednesday morning we'd do Act 1, known, having given another performance the previous night. We would run it but we could only run it a short time in the morning up to about 12.30 because at 2.30 we would do the matinee, followed by the evening performance. On Thursday we'd do Act 2, known, and then you'd have to let the actors go about two o'clock at the latest because they'd have to learn Act 3 and do the evening show. All this meant of course that if you had a stinking long part, you'd be up half the night learning your stuff. Come Friday, you'd do Act 3 in the morning, break for lunch, and in the afternoon Act 1 again because by then people would be tending to forget it. Saturday morning we would run the whole play straight through with as many props as possible but in the wrong set! Saturday afternoon there would be a matinee followed by the evening performance.

'The stage staff would get the set down and clear everything off ready for the new set. Scenic artists would work all day Sunday, painting, touching up. Monday morning in would come the stage management with all the props they'd begged, borrowed or stolen. The director would be madly trying to light it at the same time and get the sound effects right for half past two when the cast would assemble to do it as they would be doing it that night. First performance that night and the following morning, Tuesday, you'd start the next play. And so it went on, for six months at least.'

The policy of mixing ambitious plays with lighter material continued. *The Caretaker* was presented in November 1972, and the stage premiere of *The Servant* in February 1973. Three months later Charles Vance played Archie Rice in *The Entertainer*. The latter continues to be regarded as an outstanding highlight of the company's six years at the Park. It was directed by Dennis Spencer who was to be responsible for many further productions. The autumn season of 1973 included Pinter's *The Birthday Party* and Albee's *Who's Afraid of Virginia Woolf?*

Amanda Wilkins affirms that Charles Vance put on pantomimes of superb quality. The 1973 production of *Jack and the Beanstalk* included a guest star from earlier days of British cinema and stage. James Kenney was still remembered for his 1951 role of *Cosh Boy*, but here he was playing Dame Durden.

As 1974 got under way, Dennis Spencer took on more of the direction and one of his productions was *A Man For All Seasons*, which began on 12 March. As well as directing, Dennis played Thomas Cromwell. Standing out in his memory was the visit on the Saturday evening by Dame Flora Robson who had come from her home in Brighton to see it. When she went backstage afterwards, she expressed gratitude to the company for making the play 'so clear for me', which they all felt was a great compliment to a rep company.

In the week beginning 26 March, Dennis Spencer directed *The Two Mrs Carrolls*, the play that some ten years earlier had caused such headaches for the young Clive Francis as an ASM. The present company played it in the face

Telephone 21121

DEVONSHIRE PARK THEATRE EASTBOURNE

Director of Entertainments & Publicity — PETER M. BEDFORD
Deputy Director — ERNEST FULCHER

Monday. 27th May to 1st June, 1974

CHARLES VANCE

presents

THE EASTBOURNE THEATRE COMPANY

in

THE HEIRESS

by Ruth and Augustus Goetz

CHARACTERS—in order of appearance

Maria (The Parlour Maid) .... CANDYCE BRANDL
Dr. Austin Sloper .... ANTONY LINFORD
Mrs. Lavinia Penniman (his Sister) .... SUZANNE JEFFERIES
Catharine (his Daughter) .... WENDY BRIERLEY
Mrs. Elizabeth Almond (his Sister) .... IMOGEN MOYNIHAN
Marian Almond (his Niece) .... ALWYNE TAYLOR
Arthur Townsend (Marian's Fiance) .... MARTIN WIMBUSH
Morris Townsend (Arthur's Cousin) .... CHRIS WINNERA
Mrs. Montgomery (Morris's Sister) .... JOANNA SANDS

Directed by DENNIS SPENCER

Designed by RICHARD HAMMOND

of the fiercest competition. Next door at the Congress was a presentation of *A Funny Thing Happened on the Way to the Forum.* Bursting with names, the company was headed by the legend of Sgt Ernie Bilko: Phil Silvers. The take at the DPT box office must have been pitiful.

Dennis Spencer also directed the following week's production, *Intent to Murder*. This was the thriller which in the mid-Fifties had been adapted for the big screen as *Another Man's Poison* with Bette Davis and Gary Merrill. The play was written by Leslie Sands, a popular actor and playwright, perhaps best known for the title role in the television detective series, *Cluff*. Leslie Sands and his wife Pauline Williams had long been residents in Eastbourne. It was their daughter, Joanna Sands who, as we saw earlier, had spent most of her young working life backstage at the Devonshire Park Theatre for Richard Burnett's various 1960s companies. Now she was appearing onstage in many of the Charles Vance productions, including those directed by Dennis Spencer. One example was a pre-

* * *

Our Supporters' Club has just undergone a facelift. It is now called the EASTBOURNE THEATRE CLUB and it has its own committee, runs its own affairs and has a very exciting programme lined up for its members. For example, they have organised a party to go to the Chichester Festival Theatre to see *A Month in the Country;* they are entering a float in this year's Eastbourne Carnival, and they have arranged for ALAN MELVILLE to come and talk to them on 13th June. Coffee mornings, Newsletters and a Christmas Party are all in the offing. All this has been arranged in a month. Congratulations—and here's hoping you double your membership by 1975.

* * *

April 1974

sentation of *The Heiress* in May 1974, which still stands out today in the memory of production assistant Amanda Wilkins.

Intent to Murder was presented not at the DPT but at the Royal Hippodrome. This was another feature of the Charles Vance years. During those weeks earmarked for the Eastbourne Operatic and Dramatic Society and others, the Eastbourne Theatre Company transferred for the week to Seaside Road.

When asked about this aspect in 1996, Mr Vance claimed that the process did not create problems. The regular audience was loyal and was prepared to 'go the extra mile'. All the company's sets were built in the old squash courts in Devonshire Park which provided the workshop, and for the Royal Hippodrome weeks the sets were adapted as necessary.

The sense of community engendered by the repertory system and referred to earlier by Dennis Spencer continued to grow. A special note in the programme for the May production of *Verdict* recorded the development of the theatre supporters' club.

There was an emphasis 'on keeping in touch'. When, on 1 June 1974, the company saw one of its regular players, Wendy Brierley, take her leave for several months, a page was devoted in the programme to a letter she wrote about her departure. As Dennis Spencer said earlier, there was something akin to a football team following. When Mrs Charles Vance, Imogen Moynihan, returned after a spell away, in June 1974, she too was given programme space to express her thoughts.

Nor were the backstage staff left out. They were featured in the 10 June 1974 programme for *Countercrime*.

Occasionally the programme would feature a

OUR STAGE MANAGEMENT

Under the leadership of that bearded whiz-kid, Richard Lockwood, this much abused, battered crew are responsible for every stick of furniture used on the stage—for every sound effect—for every prop. Whether they are prompting the actor during rehearsal or begging a stuffed lion from a taxidermist, their work is never done . . . They are also required to be good tea makers.

Introduce them Richard!

RICHARD LOCKWOOD

First of all myself. Married with two children. Been with Charles Vance since 1970 . . . 187 productions! . . . there must have been a holiday somewhere—HELP! Beachy Head here I come.

MARGUERITE KERSHAW

Trained at Arts Educational Schools as a dancer but tripped her way into stage management. Ambition, a television director.

JONATHAN BAYLIS

Interested equally in acting and the technical side. Hopes finally to go into the film industry.

CANDYCE BRANDL

Her father escaped from Czechoslovakia in 1939. Candy was trained at Guildford Drama School. She appeared in *The Heiress* and plays Miss Johnstone in *Countercrime*.

BILL SYKES

Resident stage manager. Not strictly one of the team, but we insist on having him in our photograph. Thank you for all your hard work, Bill.

That's all Folks.

WALLINGFORD

SE,

BERKS.

7th June 1974

Dear Mr Vance,

I was happy to receive your letter of the 3rd June telling me about the annual Summer Festival of the Eastbourne Theatre. My best wishes go to all your Company on the occasion of the production of my two plays, The Hollow and Fiddlers Three. I hope that all who attend these performances will have as much enjoyment from them as I had in the writing. Good luck to all concerned in the production which I hope will prove to be a happy one.

With best wishes from my husband and myself to you and to your wife,

Yours sincerely,

Agatha Christie

Dame Agatha Christie

Charles Vance Esq
Devonshire Park Theatre

'What ever happened to....?' section and give news of company members who had moved on to other theatres. There were also many who had moved on and out of the profession altogether. A note in the 13 April programme for *Love In A Mist* made the point eloquently. 'Some, like the brief candle, flicker and are all too often forgotten.'

In all the programmes the present writer has studied covering so many periods of the theatre's history, he has been astonished at the countless names of actors and actresses who have appeared onstage for perhaps two years, if as much, and then disappeared altogether, presumably to become bank clerks, hairdressers, navvies and so on. Such an investigation gives an idea of the unemployment rate in the profession, to say nothing of the vast numbers of frustrated performers who must be at large.

Summer 1974 saw another Summer Festival involving three plays offered in continuous rotation. Two of them were by Agatha Christie, including one never yet performed in London, *Fiddlers Three*. Its presentation brought a message from the author.

By the mid-Seventies the ethos of weekly rep was being questioned generally. It was treated with increasing hostility by some producers who claimed their chances of obtaining any kind of subsidy, be it local or national, were diminished if they continued to operate the system.

Charles Vance himself had occasionally presented a play for two weeks since arriving in Eastbourne in the autumn of 1969. Usually they had been when a guest star had been booked. In October 1972, for example, Irene Handl had appeared in *Goodnight, Mrs Puffin* for a fortnight. Similarly a presentation of *Private Lives* had been mounted in February 1974. A somewhat fateful one it had proved to be. One of the players was Elizabeth Power, returning to the Park ten years after her baptism in drama student days. It was in *Private Lives* that she met for the first time the guest star, Michael Aspel.

With the 1974 Summer Festival out of the way, Charles Vance instituted a change in the autumn: fortnightly rep. He introduced the plan in the programme for *Never Too Late* on 30 September.

It must have been a gamble. The writer recalls vividly the same innovation being introduced earlier at the Palace Theatre, Westcliff-on-Sea. The regular patrons complained forcefully at no longer being able to make a weekly visit to the theatre.

> Dear Patron,
>
> The Eastbourne Theatre Company was founded on the 1st September 1969 and we are very proud that in the last five years of primarily weekly repertory we have performed for 574,932 patrons. During that time, in association with the Director of Entertainments and Publicity, Mr. Peter M. Bedford, we have introduced a number of innovations—notably the Summer Festival of Theatre which has been a great success with holidaymakers, and the establishment of an annual pantomime at the Park which now caters for some 20,000 people over the Christmas period.
>
> Mr. Bedford and I have now established a new policy which is launched with this present production: the introduction of fortnightly repertory as an integral part of Devonshire Park Theatre policy.
>
> We believe that the very high standard of production which this will enable us to present, coupled with the opportunity it will provide to have visits from distinguished guest stars in occasional productions, will further enhance the image of the Eastbourne Theatre Company and give it an appeal to a very much wider public.
>
> We hope you enjoy this, the first play under this new policy, and I am very proud to announce that in our next production, Somerset Maugham's RAIN, the role of Sadie Thompson will be played by GABRIELLE DRAKE, the star of BBC/TV's THE BROTHERS.
>
> We have a very exciting programme for the autumn, culminating in our annual pantomime, which this year will be ALADDIN, and we look forward to seeing you regularly during the season.
>
> Yours sincerely,
>
> CHARLES VANCE,
> Actor/Manager.

The advantages to the acting profession, however, were enormous. Alongside the opportunity to have more star names, the treadmill life of the weekly rep actor was suddenly improved by 100%, with that percentage of time now added to the study of his lines and character.

One of the first productions under the new system was *Hamlet*. Its director, Dennis Spencer, recalls it fondly.

'Tony Linford played Hamlet and the whole company was extremely strong. We played it at quite a speed, aiming it at sixteen year-olds. We thought we'd play it with all the zip of a gangster play really. We had marvellous costumes from Stratford and it worked a treat.'

Dennis also directed in early December Rattigan's *In Praise of Love*, for which guest star Derren Nesbitt was brought in. As with Elizabeth Power a few months earlier, he met his future spouse, Sue of the wardrobe department, during the course of his visit.

1975 began well enough with the fortnightly format now in full swing. Lynda Baron guest-starred in *Butterflies Are Free* in January, and Ian Lavender played in *The Promise* in February.

It was in March that signs began to appear that this was to be the last season of the Eastbourne Theatre Company. The programme for the production of *Who's Who* by Keith Waterhouse and Willis Hall provided clues. No longer was there an application form to join the theatre club included. A biography of one of the backstage staff recorded that Candyce Jane Brandl was not only the senior ASM but had also made a number of small appearances in productions 'and will continue to do so during the remainder of the Company's life at Devonshire Park.'

The Company

There was still the current season to work through, however, and Dennis Spencer continued to play a substantial part which included directing productions of *Look Back in Anger* and *Who Saw Him Die?* in April.

Dennis was well represented in the final Summer Festival. Not only did he act and direct, but he was also the author of one of the three rotated offerings: *Sing a Song of Murder*. Dennis Spencer was not new to writing. His comedy *What a Racket!* with Arthur Askey had played long summer seasons at Blackpool and Torquay. His *Sing a Song of Murde*r received its premiere in the 1975 Summer Festival. A photo was taken outside the theatre to mark the event, when the company could be seen to be in danger of tripping over each other's flares. Dennis Spencer is pictured fifth from the right.

Summer passed rapidly, followed by the countdown to the end, which came on Saturday 27 September 1975. The play was *The Man in Grey* by Barbara Toy and Moie Charles. It was directed by Imogen Moynihan and featured Charles Vance. Even the company's longstanding production manager, Richard Lockwood, played a part. There was a distinct whiff of everyone clambering into the lifeboat. Charles Vance addressed his customers with a long letter of farewell.

It was a bitter departure, one that still rankled more than twenty years later. The Director of Entertainments of the day had told the actor/manager – according to Charles Vance – that it was time for his caravan to move on. Speaking in 1996, Mr Vance summed up the situation. In his view he had been told in 1975 that the Devonshire Park Theatre 'needs to become Peter Bedford's touring company theatre, not Charles Vance's permanent theatre.'

Anyone with the merest knowledge of show business knows how driven it is by politics, sufficient to give the Palace of Westminster a run for its money. But there can be little doubt that the six years from 1969 provides one of the most significant periods of the Devonshire Park Theatre's history. Building on the strength of weekly repertory established in the Fifties and Sixties, the pattern had continued. A series of reputable acting squads had performed a firm body of important theatre plays along with the 'safe' work. A sense of community had grown, with greater emphasis than hitherto placed on the importance of a theatre supporters' club. A brave transition to fortnightly rep in a bid for still greater quality had also been achieved.

However, it was at such a point that the Park's twenty-three years of almost continuous repertory work came to an end. The pendulum had swung back yet again in favour of touring productions. All over Britain the rep system was declining, although Charles Vance would report twenty years later on its qualified re-emergence.

As to the man himself holding the reins throughout the Devonshire Park Theatre's final period of continuous repertory theatre, allow Dennis Spencer to have the last word.

'Charles used to wear a green corduroy jacket and carry a silver-topped cane which he swore had belonged to Henry Irving and he stood in the foyer to welcome people in. He was a great publicist and still is. Of all the reps I've been in with Charles, and they go back to 1961, this one at Eastbourne was the happiest, and I think he felt the same.'

XI

Touring With Triumph

Following Charles Vance's departure, the Devonshire Park Theatre was closed for no more than one week. During the last months of the Eastbourne Theatre Company's residence, Peter M Bedford had been busy. On behalf of Eastbourne Corporation, the Director of Entertainments had taken over policy and management of the theatre. He had achieved an agreement with Triumph Theatre Productions. This must be regarded as a coup of the time. Triumph was arguably at its highest point by the late Seventies. Formed and directed by Duncan C Weldon, Louis I Michaels and Richard Todd, the company had gained a strong reputation, responsible for placing many West End productions including several at the Theatre Royal, Haymarket.

Weldon and Michaels had created a circuit of twelve theatres around the country. Each play they presented under the Triumph banner had a guaranteed run at all twelve, which included the Devonshire Park Theatre.

The itinerary was such that the play would come to Eastbourne before going to Brighton. Eventually it was noticed that some of the Brighton

Devonshire Park Theatre
Eastbourne

Director of Entertainment & Publicity PETER M. BEDFORD
Deputy Director ERNEST FULCHER

Telephone
Administration 25252 **Box Office 21121**

Week Commencing Monday 6th October 1975

DUNCAN C. WELDON AND LOUIS I. MICHAELS
FOR TRIUMPH THEATRE (PRODUCTIONS) LTD PRESENT

PHYLLIS CALVERT
AND
RICHARD VERNON
IN
THE RELUCTANT DEBUTANTE
BY
WILLIAM DOUGLAS HOME
WITH
KATE NICHOLLS
OSMUND BULLOCK **SALLY TEMPLER**
MICHAEL MENAUGH **ESTELLE COLLINS**
AND
ALICE FRASER
DIRECTED BY
NIGEL PATRICK
Designed by John Page

fans were coming across to Eastbourne to see the plays rather than wait for them to reach Brighton. As a result the Devonshire Park's business increased consistently.

This created a political snag. Beside being a director of Triumph Productions, Louis I Michaels was the owner of the Theatre Royal, Brighton. He was displeased at what was happening, with the result that the itinerary was rearranged. All plays on the circuit went to Brighton before coming to Eastbourne.

The first production under the new arrangement was William Douglas Home's *The Reluctant Debutante* on Monday 6 October 1975. It featured one of the best loved names of the day, Phyllis Calvert.

From then on, for several years, top-drawer stars arrived in Compton Street. As Miss Calvert vacated the no 1 dressing room, Dora Bryan moved her make-up box in. An incident in one performance during the week of 13 October caused her to include it in her autobiography, *According to Dora*. The play was Alan Ayckbourn's *Relatively Speaking*. Her dog, Dougal, wandered on to the set in a quiet scene.

'Having made his entrance he then proceeded to eat all the sugar lumps on the coffee table. Simon Williams, who was in the scene with me, loved it. We were supposed to be in a garden, and after being thrown for a moment, Simon began to ad lib magnificently. "Oh, what a dear little dog," he said. "What's his name?"

Me (horrified): He's not allowed in the garden.
Simon: Why not?
Me (desperate): He'll ruin the turf.
Simon (by now enjoying himself): You mean he'll cock his leg?

Dougal was having a wonderful time, basking in the limelight. He would not go off stage and stay off, but kept returning through garden doors, stage right and stage left. Anyone but Simon would quite rightly have been extremely angry. So would Alan Ayckbourn, I imagine. The ad-libbed dialogue wasn't quite up to his standard.'

This production, incidentally, came not from Triumph but from an up-and-coming young entrepreneur by the name of Cameron Mackintosh.

The autumn of 1975 saw prestigious productions of *Sleuth* with Richard Todd and Peter Byrne; *All Things Bright and Beautiful* with Peggy Mount; and Frederick Lonsdale's *On Approval*. The latter featured Edward Woodward, Geraldine McEwan, Jennie Linden and Edward Hardwicke.

The season also saw a triumphant return. It has been recorded how a nineteen year-old June Whitfield had stage-managed *Fit For Heroes* in November 1945. Exactly thirty years later, Miss Whitfield returned with her television partner, Terry Scott, for the premiere production of *A Bed Full of Foreigners*. They had not long completed a successful tour of South Africa (where the writer had missed them by weeks in Durban, on his way home from three years in northern Zambia). Shortly after Eastbourne, the company, which included Lynda Baron and Colin Jeavons, took up residence at London's Victoria Palace where they stayed for a long run.

1976 was devoted almost entirely to Triumph touring shows but occasional productions by Michael Codron and Bill Kenwright were included. Intended for arrival in Eastbourne on its way around the country was a production of Sam Cree's *The Mating Season*. It was scheduled to open on 17 May. Its strong supporting cast included Audrey Jeans, Olga Lowe, Bill Waddington, Rosalyn Elvin and Dorothy Dampier. Two weeks earlier it had reached the Sunderland Empire. In the middle of the performance on Monday 26 April, its star, Sidney James, collapsed onstage with a massive heart attack, and the tour died with him.

A particular production stands out in the memory of the then manager of the Devonshire Park Theatre, Peter Felgate. The play booked was *My Fat Friend* starring John Inman and Anne Stallybrass. It opened on Bank Holiday Monday 31 May 1976. Because of his television work and catchphrase, 'I'm free!', John Inman was a huge box office attraction of the period.

At the time there were two box offices in the foyer. The one that presently exists was for advance bookings. The second was immediately opposite – later to serve as the confectionery kiosk – and was for 'Today's Performance only'.

On the Bank Holiday Monday, the box office opened as usual at ten o'clock in the morning. By that time two queues had already formed. They stretched around the entrance pillar and into Compton Street as far as the Buccaneer. The queue for advanced bookings did not shorten until four o'clock in the afternoon. The pattern was repeated until the Thursday; an indication, if one were needed, that it is possible for the DPT to pull the customers in.

Peter Felgate himself comes from a strong theatrical pedigree. As far back as 1924 his parents, Felgate King and Elsie Mayfair, had brought a group of entertainers to Eastbourne to perform on the pier bandstand. Shortly afterwards Felgate King opened the New Music Pavilion with his show, *The Pier Revels*. He presented three shows a year: summer season, pantomime and short Easter season. The show continued until 1935 when Clarkson Rose took over with *Twinkle*. The young Peter Felgate appeared in that show as he had done in his parents'.

Mr Felgate joined Eastbourne Corporation in 1974 and took over the management of the Royal Hippodrome Theatre where he was resident for the summer and moved to the Park for the winter months. After Charles Vance's departure the following year, he moved to the DPT as permanent manager. During the ten years he was with the Corporation/Borough Council, until his retirement, he became one of the theatre's most popular managers.

Following a lifetime as a performer or producer in show business, one of the bonuses for Peter Felgate was in renewing links with artists he had worked with.

'It was a great joy to see them in the dressing room and to have a little chat. People like Jack Hulbert and Ciss (Cicely) Courtneidge, for example. I had been in a show with them called *Over The Moon*. We did nine months in the West End and it was lovely to see them. But it was also very very sad because they were reaching the twilight end of their careers. Both of them were ill and only a shadow of their former selves. Both of them had to sit onstage and they did a sort of resumé of their lives in show business.'

The show to which Peter was referring played 4 October and week 1976 and was entitled, poignantly enough, *Once More With Music*.

Three weeks later a touch of old Hollywood came to the Devonshire Park Theatre. The title role of *Lucy Crown* was taken by the immortalised 'Baby Doll'. By then Carroll Baker had left the United States and her new home in Europe gave her the chance to make her British stage debut, which *Lucy Crown* provided.

At the same time as the country was celebrating the Queen's Silver Jubilee in June 1977, Peter Felgate recalls a coinciding production of *A Bed Full of Foreigners*, nearly two years after the original version had passed through. Playing the lead early on in his career was David Jason.

'We could all see even then that he was going to be a very big name. He was the best one I ever saw do that play and he was obviously destined for much bigger things.'

Of all the revered returnees as 'names' to the Devonshire Park Theatre, none was more welcome than the local boy who had collected autographs at the stage door twenty years earlier. On 17 October 1977 Clive Francis led the company in the Peter Coe production of *Romeo and Juliet*.

Triumph Productions continued with their programme and in November 1978 the combined cream of 1940s Rank Organisation days, Margaret

SPECIAL PRESENTATION

AT DEVONSHIRE PARK THEATRE

WEEK COMMENCING MONDAY 17th OCTOBER

Monday to Friday at 8.00 p.m. Saturday at 8.30 p.m.

Matinees: Wednesday at 2.30 p.m. and Saturday at 5.00 p.m.

MICHELE DOTRICE
DORIS HARE
EDGAR WREFORD
CLIVE FRANCIS
JOHN STONE
MARK WYNTER

IN

ROMEO AND JULIET

by WILLIAM SHAKESPEARE

WITH FULL SUPPORTING COMPANY

Tickets: £1.95, £1.75, £1.50, £1.25, £1.00, 75p

Lockwood and Phyllis Calvert, starred in Noel Coward's *Suite in Two Keys*. Appearing with them, also from the golden age of British cinema, was Robert Flemyng.

'He was another old chum,' recalls Peter Felgate. 'I always knew when Robert was in the building. I would come in an hour before curtain up to go round inspecting the theatre, making sure it was all right ready to open up. I would find Robert in the right hand passage way of the stalls flat on his back doing exercises and deep breathing, legs raised etc. He had a bad leg of course and he always did this before a performance in order to get himself relaxed and fit.'

Highlights of 1979 included Cathleen Nesbitt in *The Aspern Papers*, Leonard Rossiter in *Semi-Detached*, Paul Eddington in *She Would If She Could*, and Edward Woodward and Michelle Dotrice in *Beggar's Opera*. In the October, four years after his departure as resident actor/manager, Charles Vance presented his touring production of *Witness For The Prosecution*, directed by Dennis Spencer and starring Eunice Gayson as Romaine.

The following two years saw changes. One of the most significant was that the arrangement with Triumph Productions was petering out. Plays under their banner were no longer a regular feature. For instance, in September 1980, Christopher Timothy and Dora Bryan appeared in Walter Greenwood's *The Cure For Love* in the first Triumph presentation at the Park for ten months.

Another change, as far as manager Peter Felgate was concerned, was in the quality of play. For him two successive weeks in November 1980 provided a massive contrast. The New Vic Theatre presented *Canterbury Tales* which was followed by Bill Kenwright's tour of *Joseph and the Amazing Technicolour Dreamcoat* starring Jess Conrad. Peter Felgate reflects.

'During my latter years I began to notice that the plays and shows were getting more and more vulgar: something which I didn't approve of. The language would become quite obscene in some shows like *Canterbury Tales*. In itself the bawdiness was acceptable but they had a link man who was more or less a stand-up comic and quite filthy.

'Then there were shows like *The Rocky Horror Show* that I found difficult to accept. In fact with some of the plays I could tell after the Monday night that I was going to have trouble because a lot of the regulars felt the same way. If it became too much for me, I would retreat into the box office with the door slightly ajar so that I was available but not seen. In that way I would hope they would pass by muttering to themselves and go on their way and into the night without attacking me. Once or twice I would get caught. I couldn't come out with the argument: "Well, this is theatre and perfectly acceptable", because I agreed with their objections.

'I do remember being taken completely by surprise, and delightfully so, the first time we had *Joseph*. I still think it's one of the best of Andrew Lloyd Webber's. And of course we had the old favourites like *Salad Days*.

'You see, I was brought up in a very strict world of entertainment. The very slogan of the Fols de Rols was: "The show that any child can take its parent to". In my father's shows even further back, he would never even allow the word "lousy" in the script. So you can understand that my upbringing was as far as today's theatre is concerned, very strait-laced.'

1981 provided a variety of work at the theatre. Honor Blackman recreated Glenda Jackson's *Rose* and the Old Vic company packed the theatre to the rafters with *The Merchant of Venice*. Timothy West was Shylock and Prunella Scales was Portia. Susan Hampshire starred in Durbridge's *House Guest* and Moira Lister appeared in *The Marquise*. There was Joanna Lumley in *Private Lives*, Alfred Marks in *An Inspector Calls*, and Simon Ward in *Whose Life is it Anyway?*

The late Preston Lockwood told of how he was collected each evening by Joss Ackland to be driven to Compton Street for the week's run of *The Dresser*. One evening there was another passenger in the back seat who was coming to see the performance. As Mr Lockwood stepped into the car, he was astonished to hear Ackland say to him by way of introduction: 'Do you know Ingrid Bergman?'

On 5 October 1981 *The Kingfisher* was presented with Michael Denison and Dulcie Gray. An incident during its run is forever etched on Peter Felgate's memory.

In those days the tradition of serving tea trays at the matinee still obtained. Sometimes if the house was busy, there would be as many as one hundred trays to cope with. We have seen that in a January 1954 programme, staff member Evelyn Harmer was listed as 'Usherette, Upper Circle'. Twenty-two years later she had progressed to the number one position, right hand door of the stalls. Peter Felgate remembers her with affection and recalls that she was better known to all her fans as 'Ginger'. The Wednesday matinee for *The Kingfisher* was packed. Mr Felgate takes up the story.

'Michael Denison was a stickler for everything being done correctly. At the time I had an arrangement with Bill Sikes, the stage manager, that once the interval was clear and all the trays were out, I would give Bill the all-clear for the curtain to be rung up. To this day I marvel at how they got all the trays in and out without mishap.

'On this one occasion, Ginger had forgotten one tray, and it happened to be slap bang in the middle of the front row of the stalls. She suddenly remembered. She dashed into the auditorium. In the meantime I had given the all-clear to Bill Sikes.

'Just as Ginger was bending over to pick up the tray, with her rear towards the stage, the curtain went up. Michael Denison was already onstage about to say his first line. I hesitate to guess what went through his mind for it must have been a very unnerving sight. Ginger rapidly disappeared from the auditorium with the tray.

'At the end of the performance Mr Denison let it be known that the incident had incurred his displeasure. But it was the subject of merriment for years to come.'

The most far-reaching change saw the start of much closer involvement than hitherto by a certain production company in the summer of 1981, which has remained ever since. The company had begun eleven years earlier in the unprepossessing atmosphere of Shanklin Town Hall in out-of-season October. Two actors, John Newman and Daphne Palmer, had decided to team up professionally to form Newpalm Productions. During the Seventies they set up base camp at the Civic Theatre, Chelmsford, where they are still.

Newpalm's first work at the Devonshire Park Theatre was in October 1975 when, in association with Triumph, they presented *The Gentle Hook.* It featured Hilary Tindall and Charles Stapley and was directed by Jack Watling (whose deputy stage manager was his young son, Giles).

In March 1976, Newpalm presented *Spider's Web* with Elizabeth Larner and therein lay a strong link with the past. We have seen that Daphne Palmer had appeared in the Theatre South East production of *A Song At Twilight* in 1969. Now the tables were reversed. Returning to the DPT to appear in Newpalm's *Spider's Web* were the couple who had run the theatre throughout the Sixties: Richard Burnett and Peggy Paige. It was to be their final visit to their old work place.

1978 saw Newpalm presenting *The Unexpected Guest* with Peter Byrne. Also in the cast was Dennis Spencer who was to do increasing amounts of work with Newpalm over the ensuing years as well as keeping up his links with the various Charles Vance companies.

Other touring Newpalm productions coming the Devonshire Park's way included *Deadline* starring Max Wall – just prior to his cult popularity establishing itself – and *Blithe Spirit*, both in 1979. Portraying Elvira in the Coward play was Judy Carne, a renowned personality of the time, still enjoying a reputation as the 'Sock it to me' girl from *Rowan and Martin's Laugh In*, made in Hollywood. Miss Carne was also still known at the time as the ex Mrs Burt Reynolds.

By the summer of 1981, therefore, Newpalm was established and it presented the first of its many summer seasons to Eastbourne audiences. On 29 June *Beyond a Joke* opened for twelve weeks. The strong cast included Deborah Watling, daughter of Jack, and her husband Nick Field, son of Sid! The star of *Beyond a Joke* was Arthur Lowe who had become a much-loved national institution as Captain Mainwaring in *Dad's Army*. It was a theatrical coup of its time, for both Newpalm and Eastbourne, to secure his services for so long a season. Yet again Peter Felgate was able to renew an old friendship.

'We had been together in *Call Me Madam* at the London Coliseum. Arthur played a small part, one of the senators. And again when he came to the

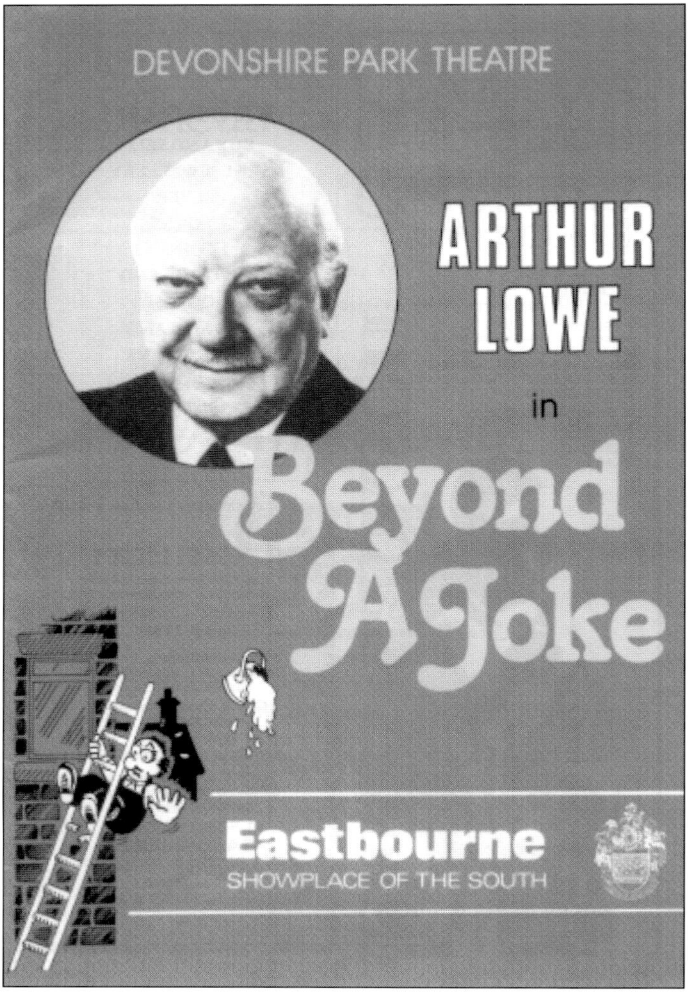

Summer 1981

Devonshire Park he was getting on towards the end of his career. For some reason unknown to us, he was always dropping off to sleep. He would even do so onstage, so much so that we nicknamed him The Dormouse. Sadly we didn't realise at the time that this was the onset of an illness that was eventually to prove fatal.'

The end came a few months later. Following the summer season, Mr Lowe appeared again at the Devonshire Park Theatre in R C Sheriff's *Home At Seven*, in April 1982. It was elsewhere during the national tour that Arthur Lowe collapsed and died.

Also appearing in *Beyond a Joke* was the seasoned jobbing actress, Peggy Ashby. She had a pet poodle called 'Ashby'. She also had a formidable personality and would not countenance the suggestion that Ashby be forbidden entry into the theatre. Dennis Spencer can vouch for it.

'If you were on tour with Peggy, often they'd say at the theatre: "She's not coomin' in 'ere with that dog", and I'd say: "Well, that's up to you." But Peggy had a very determined look and the dog was always under her arm. She would head for the stage door like a galleon with all guns firing. I've seen the strongest of stage door-keepers quail and say: "Your key, Miss Ashby", and the dog would go in.'

Newpalm returned the following summer to be in residence from 28 June to 2 October 1982. This time it was a split season, the first five weeks taken up by Patricia Phoenix and Anthony Booth in *The Unexpected Guest*. Pat and Tony, as they were affectionately known, came to be Newpalm regulars. Subsequent summer seasons found them performing in Mel Dinelli's *The Man*, and in Agatha Christie's *Spider's Web*.

John Newman recalls Patricia Phoenix as the true professional. She would be the first to distribute leaflets on the pier, encouraging potential customers. If they asked her for an autograph, she would gently refuse but suggest they came along to the show and she would gladly give them a signed photograph afterwards at the stage door.

The remaining two months of the 1982 summer season saw the ever popular John Inman back in *My Fat Friend*.

Meanwhile the year's tours included the Oxford Playhouse Company in *Macbeth*, Lionel Blair in *Once In A Lifetime* (which had just scored a huge hit by the RSC at the Aldwych Theatre) and Simon Gray's *Quartermaine's Terms* with Michael Williams.

The satirical play about the Thatchers, *Anyone For Denis?*, had enjoyed a successful run at the Whitehall Theatre but had collapsed with the onset of the Falklands War in the spring of 1982. It was thus released for tour and came to Eastbourne in October. In the same month Brian Murphy appeared as *Sweeney Todd* and Maxine Audley starred in *Relatively Speaking*.

1983 saw Newpalm Productions taking up even more time at the Devonshire Park Theatre. They continued to present the occasional touring production, such as *Habeas Corpus* with Jack Douglas, in the spring. Their summer season of twelve weeks was now established, with the first month of the current season taken up by Jack Watling starring in *Verdict*. The second show was a certainty for success with Eastbourne audiences. Taken directly from the television series, *Last of the Summer Wine* starred Bill Owen, Peter Sallis and Jane Freeman.

Newpalm then provided additional entertainment for the winter months, either side of Christmas. Their first period under the label Newpalm Repertory Company began on 15 November 1983. It ran for four weeks and the plays were *Time and Time Again*, *The Late Edwina Black*, *Towards Zero* and *The Ghost Train*: all standard repertory fare. A further four-week season began on 7 February 1984. *An Inspector Calls*, *Ten Little Indians* (at the halfway house

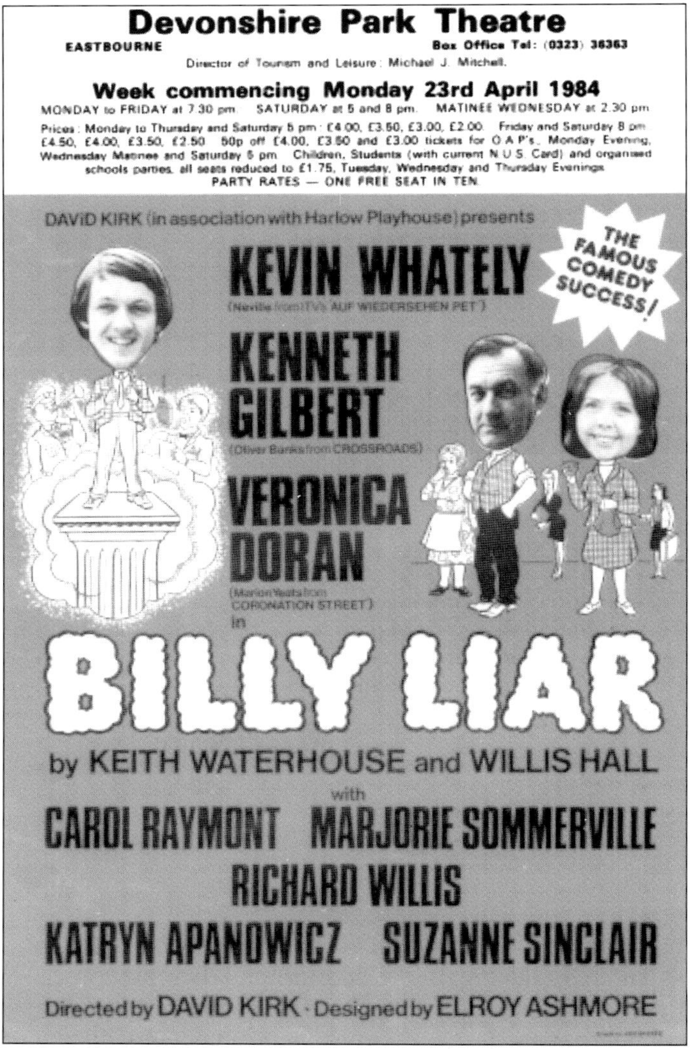

of political correctness), *Relatively Speaking* and *Trap For a Lonely Man* were the selected pieces.

The new procedure helped cushion the regret manager Peter Felgate voiced that the theatre remained dark for so long.

'I put in a plea many times for us to hold the pantomime in the Devonshire Park because I felt it was a much more suitable place to have the Christmas show. It was much more intimate, the children had much more involvement there, and when Charlie Vance did all his pantomimes in the theatre, they were a great success. But during my time it was decided that the

Congress was favourite so it wasn't until much later, after I'd left, that the pantomime returned to the Park.'

It followed, therefore, that although, up to the end of the Charles Vance era, the theatre remained open throughout the year, the bleak months of darkness had now become a feature. The innovation of the Newpalm Repertory Company winter seasons did much to alter the situation.

Among Peter Felgate's memories are four stalwart usherettes, all long-serving staff members. We have already heard about Evelyn 'Ginger' Harmer. The quartet was completed by Ethel Hyde, Jean Collard and Peggy Raine.

'Two further members of this great team who were there for so many years were Eileen Sharpe and Dee Barrow, the latter of whom still is of course. Eileen ran the confectionery kiosk and did all the catering and ice creams and organised them all with utmost efficiency. Dee runs the bar.'

Mr Felgate also paid tribute to some backstage staff.

'Bill Sikes was a stage manager very much of the old school, a strict disciplinarian. No drink was allowed to be consumed backstage by any of the staff during a performance and he generally ran a very tight ship.

'It was a fine unit and nearly all the touring managements were very glad to come to the Devonshire Park Theatre because they knew they would be in the hands of a most efficient backstage staff.

'Chief electrician was Geoff Stanfield, who had been there since Richard Burnett's days in the Sixties. A brilliant man all round, if slightly unpredictable! Geoff was succeeded by Ray Grove and in my time at the theatre they rewired and relocated new lighting and sound boxes.

'During one of the winter breaks when the theatre was closed, we reseated the entire theatre. This was under the general supervision of David Lake and he and I worked together on the plans.'

By the time of his retirement in 1984, Peter Felgate had developed an extensive knowledge of the geographical nature of the Devonshire Park Theatre.

'There's an area underneath the auditorium whereby you can go down a passageway and walk the entire breadth of the theatre below the stalls. The Fire Brigade used to come regularly to use it as a test area for their firemen to do training and drill in the pitch black with their gas masks on.

'You will appreciate that because it was an old building owned by the Corporation, it had to be regularly inspected. This was done by a great friend of mine who was the Buildings Inspector at the time, Ken Meech. Ken and I used to get together twice a year and we went to all sorts of interesting places within the building. Two of these were up the Italianate towers either side of the theatre. Where he found a crack, Ken would place a small piece of glass across it. This was so that when he came back in six months' time, he could readily tell whether there had been any movement because the glass itself would have cracked.'

The Devonshire Park Theatre moved steadily towards its one hundredth birthday and Peter Felgate took his leave, not without disillusionment at some of the plays now presented. For him there was glass cracking in the onstage material as well as in the Italianate towers.

Nonetheless, Mr Felgate describes the time overall as 'a very wonderful ten years spent in a very wonderful theatre.' He considers he left behind a dedicated band of people, backstage and front-of-house, to take the Devonshire Park Theatre into its second century.

XII

Centenary Plus

The evening of 2 June 1984 was a Saturday. The one hundredth anniversary of the theatre's opening coincided with the last performance of *Children of a Lesser God*, the study of a deaf woman in the modern world, which starred Jean St Clair and Ron Aldridge. Two evenings later the Devonshire Park Theatre began its second century with Royce Ryton's thriller, *The Voices*, featuring Peter Adamson, Derren Nesbitt and Brigitte Kahn.

ARE YOU A FRIEND YET?....

Friends of the Devonshire Park Theatre

AIMS: To provide an opportunity for Theatregoers to meet socially, regularly throughout the year to encourage interest in the Theatre generally and the Devonshire Park in particular.

To meet visiting artistes occasionally and extend the 'Hand of Friendship across the Footlights'.

PRIVILEGES: "First Nighters" - a major concession on first night Theatre Tickets.

Further concessions to all Members for some performances at The Congress and Royal Hippodrome Theatres.

ANNUAL MEMBERSHIP: Single........£5.00 Joint Husband/Wife £6.00

Forms available from the Box Office

FURTHER SHOWS FOR YOUR PLEASURE...

AT THIS THEATRE...
Week commencing Monday 7th May

Geoffrey
Coronation Street
EDDIE YATES
Hughes
&
Dilys
Watling

in Charles Dyers Famous Romatic Comedy
RATTLE OF A SIMPLE MAN

Work commencing Monday 21st May
Eastbourne Operatic and Dramatic Society presents...

ABSURD PERSON SINGULAR

by
Alan Ayckbourn

The centenary year was innovative. By the summer a new manager had been appointed and was making his mark. Roger Neil had spent several years as an actor and had come to Eastbourne to take on the Royal Hippodrome before moving to the Park. His seven-year period of office – before taking on the general managership of the Theatre Royal, Brighton – provided ample evidence of his enthusiasm for all aspects of the theatre. He was concerned in equal measure for his audiences, his staff and visiting companies. Mr Neil also lent his full support to a project that began life in 1984 and was to prove long lasting in a way similar previous efforts had not. We return briefly to Roger Neil's predecessor, Peter Felgate, who recalls its beginnings.

'A month or two before I retired, Mike Ramsden – who was then Entertainments Manager of Eastbourne Theatres – came to me and asked what I thought about forming a Friends of the Devonshire Park Theatre society.

'I said I thought it was a very good idea, so Mike asked me to cobble something together and I immediately contacted Spencer Freeman who was the annual Arts Festival director and a great friend of mine to see what we could discuss. We enlisted the aid of David and Mary Watkins who were great regular fans of the theatre and already belonged to the Theatregoers' Club of Great Britain. They had some knowledge of the rules and regulations.'

The Friends were born. The first appeal for like-minded spirits went out in the programme for *The Winslow Boy*, with Marius Goring, directed by Jeremy Sinden, in the week beginning 30 April 1984. Spencer Freeman became the first Chairman and saw the Friends through the initial years.

Since the early days the Friends have raised funds for a variety of refurbishments and floral displays. At the time of publication, a major project is planned for the restructuring of the foyer, eventually to take in facilities for the disabled, including the installation of a lift.

Perhaps the most significant area of help has been in that relating to the hard-of-hearing and visually impaired. This came in two stages, beginning with an Induction Loop System and replaced in the Nineties by an Audio Description System. The headsets for the latter serve the two disabilities.

The Audio Description System necessitates a volunteer force of Describers, recruited from the Friends. They work in pairs and on Friday evenings and Saturday matinees, non or partially sighted theatre-goers can listen to the play and, through the headsets, receive a description of the set, characters and, where necessary, action. The pair on duty are involved in a substantial amount of work during their week's shift. They spend several evenings at performances to familiarise themselves with the content and make notes, devising their own sub-scripts if desired. All Describers are trained and operate a rota system of duty. The Devonshire Park Theatre is the only one in the country offering the scheme every week.

In order to raise funds for the various pursuits, a series of coffee mornings, as well as the annual Theatrical Garden Party, are held.

The Friends have adopted three Patrons: Windsor Davies in 1989, the Duke of Devonshire two years later, and Brian Murphy in 1993.

A substantial Friends' programme is undertaken each year, incorporating Patrons' and other lunches, afternoon teas and annual dinner. A variety of speakers has been enlisted for these occasions and have included George Elrick, Clive Francis, Kathy Staff, Margaret Ashcroft and Jack Watling. Other social evenings, dances, theatre visits and highly popular weekend trips continue to feature in the programme.

The Friends enjoyed a surge of support when a 50% discount was instituted on all first night seats. The membership increased to three thousand and Monday evenings were heavily supported. The discount was reduced to 25% and membership of the Friends fell to a third of its high point number.

One claim of the time was that if people only became Friends for what they could get, they were not true Friends. The counter argument hinged on an observation made by former manager Peter Felgate when he spoke of the several benefits of beginning a week's run with a full receptive house.

Full receptive houses were to prove increasingly elusive as the DPT journeyed into its second century. The 80s and 90s saw many changes in the entertainment world with several theatres in southern England in such difficulty as to be in danger of closing altogether. Farnham, Guildford and Leatherhead were all at risk at one time or another.

Eastbourne has so far remained unique in the age of stringency and newer political theory. It has a population of fewer than ninety thousand, yet still boasts four theatre venues. Not all are open outside the holiday season, but their upkeep is still required.

Three of the venues are neighbours, sufficiently close for the area in which they stand to be known as Eastbourne's theatreland. The Devonshire Park is the third in the line. Often its evening performances compete with a Saturday night of alternative comedy at the Winter Garden or the variety of orchestral concerts, musicals and single performance dates at the 1,800-seater Congress Theatre.

Eastbourne therefore has a small population relative to other towns which have their own theatre, let alone four theatres. The catchment area is also reduced. Within those confines is a large percentage of the local population that is no longer interested in regular attendance at the theatre. There is of course no reason why they should be, any more than there ought to be a natural willingness to attend football matches or indulge in ballroom dancing.

The effect on audience figures, however, can be significant. Even in the cases of highly prestigious productions, numbers can be down, sometimes disastrously so. In May 1994 Jenny Seagrove starred as Annie Sullivan in *The*

Miracle Worker, directed by Richard Olivier. On one particular evening she played to fewer than one hundred people.

In March 1996, after the first performance of an impeccable production of Barry England's *Conduct Unbecoming*, its leading actor, Andrew Lancel, expressed considerable surprise to the writer that the theatre was not packed, as it had been throughout its tour thus far.

A similar fate was bestowed a month later in the week that George Chakiris arrived to portray Edward Rochester in *Jane Eyre*. It was to cause its producer, Charles Vance, to declare that 'bringing a production to the Devonshire Park Theatre is a luxury I can no longer afford.'

Other forces are at work. The advent of the touring production has increased quality of product, with more time available for content and performance development than was the case in the days of perpetual rush to get one rep production out one week after another. The community spirit, however, has necessarily disappeared. Not only do audiences no longer have their actors in their midst for months or even years on end, nurturing that sense of ongoing support for them, which Dennis Spencer and Gerald Sim spoke about in earlier chapters. Stage crews are also constantly faced with different company crews week after week, rendering the establishment of long-term working relationships impossible.

Particular criticism of the Devonshire Park Theatre was voiced by Mike Alfreds, artistic director of Cambridge Theatre Company, later to become Method and Madness. Writing in 1993, he said:

'I hope we'll be back to Eastbourne but the theatre – which is beautiful in itself – is very impersonally run from the local council offices. Working in it you get the feeling nobody really cares about it or what goes on in it. Compared with the other theatres we tour to, it's totally without life. During the day the foyers and bars etc of most other venues are a hive of activity.'

We shall see later how, the following year, the Theatrical Management Association took a different view. Furthermore, any reader who has come this far in the book will know that indifferent audience figures, while by no means palatable, are nothing new, and there was still plenty about which to be positive during the Eighties and Nineties. Mention has already been made, for example, of the increasing strength of support in a diversity of ways that has grown from the establishment of the Friends of the Devonshire Park Theatre.

Newpalm Productions decided to cease their winter rep operations but during their penultimate month's offering in November 1984, a special ceremony took place. This was designed to mark the centenary year. A chandelier that had previously hung in the Grand Hotel was unveiled in the auditorium.

Newpalm completed their last four-week winter season in February 1985, but the summer output continued. That year's season saw three plays stretching over a longer period. The middle of the three was an unqualified success. Eric Sykes starred in *Run For Your Wife* from 8 July to 7 September to consistently busy houses. Dick Ray provided the summer fare in 1986 but Newpalm returned the following year and have held the contract ever since.

Partly perhaps as a result of the entrepreneurial times, the period saw the sprouting of a number of theatre companies formed by actors. Reference has been made to the Cambridge Theatre Company. They brought to Eastbourne outstanding productions of *The Game of Love and Chance* by Pierre Marivaux in 1992, and in the following year Philip Osment's *The Dearly Beloved* and *Les Enfants du Paradis*, which featured Caroline Quentin as Garance.

Joanna Hole and Eric Standidge formed Co-Producers and brought David Hare's thriller *Knuckle* to the DPT in May 1987. In the following year they presented Ben Robertson as Macbeth.

The British Actors' Theatre Company prided itself on not having a director for any of its productions. When their *Taming of the Shrew* arrived in December 1987, the programme clearly stated the production was 'managed' by Peter Woodward. His brother Tim played Petruchio and Kate O'Mara was Katherine. Kate O'Mara tells how she helped to create the company. Following her two-year stint in *Dynasty*, she was prised away from Hollywood to do *King Lear* for Anthony Quayle's company. In the cast was Peter Woodward who led a hardy group on a twelve-mile route march across the Pennines during a free weekend. On the march Woodward asked O'Mara if she would be interested in forming a company. The British Actors' was born. Following several successful productions, the company ran aground on a Scandinavian tour when the entrepreneur involved failed to pay up. Only in 1997 did the company recover sufficiently to continue its work. The episode illustrates the pitfalls involved.

Corpus Productions came to play a part in the life of the Park in the late Eighties and early Nineties, and to form a certain bond with the Friends of the Theatre. The company, formed in 1989, brought *My Fat Friend*, *Deadly Replay, Rattle of a Simple Man* and *Murder Without Crime* to Eastbourne. On the company's origins, its founder Roger Tolliday commented: 'I have often been asked why, as an actor, I decided to form a theatrical company. That's simple, it seemed a natural progression.'

Vanessa Ford clearly felt the same. Not content with one production at a time, her company developed a system of presenting two plays per week. In November 1984, *Romeo and Juliet* did a split week with *A Man For All Seasons*. The following year *Macbeth* was coupled with *Rosencrantz and Guildenstern Are Dead*. In 1986 *King Lear* arrived in company with *The Importance of Being Earnest*.

The advent of a new type of thriller emerged during the period. Mention has been made of David Hare's *Knuckle*. In addition, the Devonshire Park was treated to a series of modern themes written in 'thriller' format with believable characters. A clear example was *Pack of* Lies by Hugh Whitemore, described as 'an intriguing, hypnotic and true thriller'. It lived up to its publicity in a May 1985 production with Miriam Karlin as Helen Kroger and George Sewell and Lana Morris as her neighbours, the Jacksons. *Inside Job* by Brian Clemens made an impact with its setting on the Costa del Crime and with its various themes including the controversy surrounding vigilanteism. Its star, Giles Watling, still nurtures hopes of taking the play on. He brought it to the Park in 1993.

A Canadian writer, Roger S Moss, created a trilogy of thrillers set in an old remote house. The first two, *Nightmare* and *Nightfright*, came to Eastbourne in the early Nineties to play to considerable impact. Both featured David Kershaw, the first starring Peter Byrne, the second Colin Baker.

By the Nineties, Newpalm Productions had established their month of 'Murder, Mystery and Suspense' preceding their summer seasons. There will always be a market for the Christie and Durbridge thrillers, which are the ingredients of the 'Murder' season. The one-dimensional aspect of their characters, however, does show up even more when compared with the newer examples of the genre. They lend even greater focus to the worth of the occasional classic thriller that is still of substance in the modern era and worthy of regular revival.

Tony Clayton's production of *Gaslight* scored a hit in April 1986, starring Patrick Mower and Peter Gilmore. The unlikely choice of Bernard Herrman's music from Hitchcock's *Psycho* successfully created the highest tension. It was *Gaslight* that Newpalm selected for one of its 1997 summer presentations.

Patrick Hamilton's thriller captures the psychological suffocation endured by a Victorian woman, which touches a revitalised nerve today. The Devonshire Park Theatre has not been without its share of plays pointing up concerns of women and the effect of their mutual support.

In April 1994 a touring production of *The Cemetery Club* came to Eastbourne. It starred Millicent Martin, Anne Charleston and Carmen Silvera. It made a strong impact on its audiences. At the first night reception it was noted how the script had brought tears and laughter together as to render them inseparable.

Equally memorable, in April 1995, was *Lunch Girls*, featuring Sylvia Syms, Gemma Craven and Jan Harvey. The delving into the lives of the women was painful, as with the shared grief of the bereaved wives in *The Cemetery Club*.

Neither play reached the West End, possibly indicating how a regional theatre is often at an advantage. Significant new work can be seen even though a money man along the line considers it unworthy of national recognition.

One production that did go to the West End captured the hearts of

Eastbournians as it did in all other places where it toured. *Marlene* opened the 1997 season at the Park to an acclaim that had most people passing around the all-important word of mouth following the first night. Many considered it a privilege to be able to witness the pinnacle performance of Sian Phillips' career. The cast of three unfolded another story of female resilience, in the tenderest of scripts by Pam Gems.

A glance over the programmes of the Eighties and Nineties shows a greater diversity of play arguably than at any time in the theatre's history. Inspired casting brought Peter Byrne and Joe Brown together for *Sleuth*, Jill Gascoigne, Michael Craig and Arthur English in Shaw's *Candida*, both in the centenary year.

Gert 'N Daisy, Their Musical told the story of two great music hall artistes, Elsie and Doris Waters. They were portrayed by Sylvia Syms and Rosemary Leach. Miss Elsie Waters, then in her nineties, travelled from her Steyning home to see it.

In the same year, 1985, Raymond Briggs' controversial *When The Wind Blows* came to the Park, featuring John Nettleton and his wife Deidre Doone. The writer was present at the Wednesday matinee to count eleven people including himself in the stalls. The local press reviewer, the late John Taylor-Byrne, took exception to the representation of an elderly couple with limited intelligence caught up in the imminence of nuclear war. The counter argument was that in using a cartoon approach, the horror of the incident was pointed up more graphically than it would have been by naturalistic means.

A touring version of *Blood Brothers* starring Kiki Dee came to the Devonshire Park in April 1988. At the time of publication, the same production by Bill Kenwright is still playing at the Phoenix Theatre, London.

Blood Brothers was preceded a fortnight earlier by Donald Sinden's one-man performance as Oscar Wilde at the latter end of his life in Paris, *Diversions and Delights*.

Another century was celebrated in March 1992: the one hundredth anniversary tour of *Charley's Aunt*. The tour featured Mark Curry as Lord Fancourt Babberley, backed up by Patrick Cargill, Gabrielle Drake and Frank Windsor. It played to packed houses.

1992 also saw the intriguing Ruth Rendell mystery, *The House of Stairs* with Anita Harris. A year later the Bristol Old Vic arrived with the unforgettable *Driving Miss Daisy* starring June Barrie and Don Warrington.

On Sunday 31 October 1993, Dirk Bogarde gave to a packed house an evening of readings from his numerous volumes of autobiography. A poignant moment occurred in a question-and-answer session when an elderly gentleman disclosed that he had once acted with Sir Dirk's mother in a Sussex amateur society.

Given the amount of life energy in the Devonshire Park Theatre spanning more than a century, it is perhaps not surprising that evidence of 'another world' would emerge within its precincts.

For a long time Geoffrey Stanfield, chief electrician in the Sixties and

Seventies, was the only claimant to a sighting of a ghost. It took the form of a gentleman violinist in white tie and tails who was seen in the stalls. There have been sightings since then by two other theatre personnel, including a current member of staff. Neither had knowledge of Mr Stanfield's claims. Both have given the same description of the gentleman, apparently discovered in the theatre at lock-up time after the customers had left.

In the mid-Nineties a second apparition emerged to an usherette, Enid 'Nid' Barnes, who arrived in November 1995 to take up a position in the work station defined as Opposite Main Door Stalls. Nid claims that her 'friend', whom she has christened Mary-Ellen, played tricks on her at first, hiding sugar lumps, spoons and any items related to the setting up of coffee trays for interval customers. Slowly over time, she has become a help rather than hindrance. Nid is convinced Mary-Ellen was her long-ago predecessor. Most vivid in Nid's account is Mary-Ellen's appearance.

'We are of similar height, and we both have long hair, though she appears to have mousey or blonde tresses upswept and pinned. My uniform is black and white. Hers appears to be just black: a high-necked dress, fitted to the waist with long cuffed puff sleeves. The skirt is gathered at the back-waist and does not quite touch the floor. I have never seen her feet, but can assume that like me she wears black leather footwear. Strangely, since our uniforms changed from navy blue suits with open-necked blouses to the tie-necked, puff sleeved white blouses, checked waistcoats and black skirts that we now have, Mary-Ellen has been far more sociable to me. It is as if now I am obeying her dress code and that makes me acceptable to her Edwardian, or perhaps even Victorian, sense of correctness.'

Nid Barnes is convinced that all Mary-Ellen wants is recognition of her presence. Once she knows she is in the presence of friends she will leave them alone.

'Sometimes I catch a glimpse of my silent guardian as she looks wistfully across the empty seats, maybe remembering days of a by-gone age with sounds we cannot hear of theatre-goers, waiting in anticipation for the show to start.'

The present writer can claim to have been present when an even more substantial ghost was laid to rest.

For several seasons a large moth had survived against the odds and had made frequent appearances, motivated by strong stage lighting. During the week of 3 November 1986, Ian Liston's Hiss and Boo Company brought a touring production of a play based on the board game, *Cluedo*, to the DPT. At a particular point, two of its stars, Trevor Bannister and Christopher Biggins, were onstage. Bannister had a revolver in his hand loaded with blanks. The moth appeared and caused havoc with the developing tension. From the settee where he was sitting, Biggins started chortling and pointed out what the audience was laughing at behind Bannister's back. Bannister took careful aim at the moth and fired. Biggins rolled off the settee in an uncontrollable heap. As the moth flew away, Bannister declared in deadly seriousness: 'I bet it was Henry Irving.' The house erupted. The moth has never reappeared.

The repertory days of the Fifties and Sixties had inspired several marriages. Now a long summer season was to do the same. One of the Friends' patrons, Brian Murphy, starred in *Wife Begins At Forty* in the summer of 1991 and met his co-star, Linda Regan. The couple became engaged.

The sense of goodwill continued. The rock-solid front-of-house staff carried on working with Roger Neil and then with Lisa Baron when she took over the general managership of the Park. In 1994 the efforts paid off in a prestigious result.

The Theatrical Management Association gathered in Manchester to present the annual Martini Regional Theatre Awards. Sheila Hancock was voted Best Actress for *Gypsy* at the West Yorkshire Playhouse. Alan Cumming won Best Actor for *Hamlet*. The Best Touring Production was declared as Theâtre de Complicité's *The Three Lives of Lucy Cabrol*.

The award for Most Welcoming Theatre went to the Devonshire Park Theatre, Eastbourne, whose ticket booth, observed the Daily Telegraph, cheekily or cynically, 'outdoes Concorde's check-in for toothy smiles'.

It could well be argued that it was also the several decades of service by the front-of-house staff led by chief usherette Ethel Hyde which created the special feeling of a personalised welcome on each visit to the theatre. The serving of coffee and biscuits on trays to theatre-goers in the interval continues to the present day along with the enthusiasm accompanying the procedure.

A touching moment occurred on the fiftieth anniversary of VE Day in 1995. On that Monday night, a production began for the week of *Don't Dress For Dinner*, featuring Marti Caine in her own sadly last appearance at the Park. At the end of the performance her co-star, Lionel Blair, stepped forward to complete what had been an hilarious evening. Mr Blair calmed the atmosphere to recall his, and his sister Joyce's, memories of VE Night in 1945. Then he asked the audience to stand with the cast for two minutes' silence. The audience responded, and one could have heard a pin drop. Then the familiar recording of the National Anthem struck up to herald the end of the silence. For once the audience joined in, comfortably and without embarrassment, in singing 'God Save the Queen'. Mr Blair was thanked warmly in the bar afterwards for bringing his audience to the end of a poignant day.

It has been recorded how pantomime left the Devonshire Park Theatre after the end of the Charles Vance era. It was to be ten years before the theatre reopened for Christmas, and the occasion appeared to be a singular event. The yuletide season of 1985 was significant for all three major theatre venues in

Eastbourne. The Congress was closed for the first time in years. The Royal Hippodrome Theatre was opened for the first time in decades. This was the period when the Tivoli Performing Arts Centre was flourishing and Mark Brewer spread his wings across Seaside Road to present his own production of *Cinderella*, directed by Richard Cheshire.

As a contrast, the Devonshire Park Theatre took on Piers Chater Robinson's *Dracula, or a Pain in the Neck*. The blood and gore, albeit presented tongue-in-cheek, caused a stir among the coach parties anticipating a traditional Christmas show, but the audience at which it was aimed expressed high commendation for the production.

A further seven years passed before the Park opened its doors again in late December, and it was another production of *Cinderella* that did it. The posters went up in the autumn proclaiming that Dora Bryan would be Fairy Godmother and Ross Kemp would make his panto debut as Buttons. In the event *EastEnders* would not release him from sortin' things at the Queen Vic and Dexter Fletcher was recruited.

The experiment was a success and due recognition was given to the warmth of the DPT as conducive to the atmosphere. Pantomime therefore returned home where it had been established by Murray King and Clark for thirty years from near the beginning of the century.

In common with all theatres the Devonshire Park faces a new millennium and ever changing forms of – and technologies in – the world of entertainment. Let us end by contrasting two extremes of time.

Consider any one of the actors who appeared in *The Day After The Wedding* on the opening night, 2 June 1884. There would have been no opportunity for him to seek employment in any other dramatic media. There was no video, no television, no radio. Even the first shaky attempts at commercial silent film-making were still a decade away. Insofar as any other work existed, it would have been in another theatre, after the style of the music-hall turns touring several venues in the one evening. To do that, our actor would have had to avail himself of a horse-drawn cab.

Compare the situation at the same theatre 104 summers later. Giles Watling was appearing for three months in *Noises Off*. But that was not all. Still enjoying his success as Oswald the vicar in the television sit-com, *Bread*, he had to make himself available to film a further series in the north of England. Mr Watling described the routine he undertook for part of the summer of 1988.

'I would play at the Devonshire Park Theatre in the evening, grab a couple of hours' sleep, drive to Gatwick and get a helicopter to Heathrow. Then I'd get the plane to Manchester and on the flight I'd learn the day's script while having breakfast. At Manchester I was picked up by car to go to Liverpool. I'd be on set ready to start by eight in the morning. I'd do the filming and have to clear Liverpool by about four in the afternoon to do the whole lot in reverse in order to be back in Eastbourne for the evening performance.'

A century is a long time in entertainment. Yet one element remains as true now as it did in 1884, and it is best summed up by Mike Alfreds, director of the 1992 production, *The Dearly Beloved.*

'A theatre company is nothing without its audience.'